A Flea in Her Ear

A Farce

Georges Feydeau

Translated by
John Mortimer

Samuel French - London
New York - Toronto - Hollywood

ISBN 0 573 01148 6

Please see page iv for further copyright information.

A FLEA IN HER EAR

Presented by The National Theatre at The Old Vic on 8 February 1966, with the following cast of characters:

(in order of their appearance)

CAMILLE CHANDEBISE	*Edward Hardwicke*
ANTOINETTE PLUCHEUX	*Sheila Reid*
ETIENNE PLUCHEUX	*Robert Lang*
DR FINACHE	*Kenneth Mackintosh*
LUCIENNE HOMENIDES DE HISTANGUA	*Anne Godley*
RAYMONDE CHANDEBISE	*Geraldine McEwan*
VICTOR EMMANUEL CHANDEBISE	*Albert Finney*
ROMAIN TOURNEL	*John Stride*
CARLOS HOMENIDES DE HISTANGUA	*Frank Wylie*
EUGÉNIE	*Petronella Barker*
AUGUSTIN FERAILLON	*Michael Turner*
OLYMPE	*Margo Cunningham*
BAPTISTIN	*Keith Marsh*
HERR SCHWARZ	*Peter Cellier*
POCHE	*Albert Finney*

GUESTS AT THE HOTEL COQ D'OR
  Janie Booth, Maggie Riley, David Hargreaves, Christopher Timothy Lewis Jones

The Play directed by Jacques Charon

Designed by ANDRÉ LEVASSEUR

SYNOPSIS OF SCENES

ACT I

The drawing-room of the Chandebises' house in the Boulevard Malesherbes, Paris

ACT II

The Hotel Coq d'Or in Montretout

ACT III

The Chandebises' drawing-room

Time—the early 1900s

ACT I

Scene—*The drawing-room of the Chandebises' house in the Boulevard Malesherbes. Afternoon.*

French windows R open on to a balcony. The main entrance is up C, and consists of double doors leading to a hallway and corridors to R and L. There are doors to inner rooms up RC, up LC and down L. There are doors to inner rooms up RC, up LC and down L. The fireplace is up L.

When the Curtain *rises,* Camille *is discovered standing by the filing cabinet up* LC. *His cleft palate makes his speech almost impossible to understand.* Antoinette *enters up* RC, *moves to Camille, taps his shoulder, and kisses him.*

Camille (*moving down stage*) Hare foo. Please, please be careful!
Antoinette. Calm down. The family's out.
Camille. Hoh, yes . . .
Antoinette. Come on. Give us a kiss. Well, wake up!

(*Voices are heard off up* C. Camille *exits up* L. Antoinette *moves to the door up* R. Etienne *enters up* C, *ushering in* Finache)

Etienne. Come along in, Doctor.

(Finache *enters up* C, *moves to the table* L *and puts his hat, stick and gloves on the table*)

(*To Antoinette*) What're *you* up to?
Antoinette. Me?
Etienne. You!
Antoinette. I came . . .
Etienne. Go on.
Antoinette. To ask about dinner.
Etienne. When the family's out! Back to your hot stove and bend over it! We don't have cooks in the drawing-room.
Antoinette. But . . .
Etienne. Out!

(Antoinette *exits up* C, *closing the doors*)

Finache. The Lord and Master.
Etienne (*crossing down* R) That's the way to treat them. If you're not in charge of them they're in charge of you. And I'm not having that!
Finache. Excellent!
Etienne. You know, Doctor. That little wife of mine's as faithful as a poodle, but as jealous as a tiger. She comes in here to spy on me! She's got some strange idea—about me and the housemaid . . .
Finache. How very strange . . .
Etienne (*moving* C) Me? A housemaid? Really.

FINACHE. Ridiculous! (*Moving* C) If your master's not at home . . .

ETIENNE. Don't worry. I've got time to kill—I'll keep you company.

FINACHE. I don't want to impose . . .

ETIENNE. On my good nature?

FINACHE. Certainly.

ETIENNE. Think nothing of it.

FINACHE (*bows ironically*) When will he be back?

ETIENNE. Quarter of an hour—at least.

FINACHE (*picking up his hat and stick*) Oh, in that case . . . However delightful your conversation——

ETIENNE. Too kind . . .

FINACHE. —pleasure isn't everything. I've got a patient to see. Must finish him off.

ETIENNE. Oh . . .

FINACHE. What? Oh, no—thank you very much. I'm cutting my visit short, not my patient's life. Back in a quarter of an hour . . . (*He moves up* C)

ETIENNE (*moving up* C) I must let you go.

FINACHE. It's so hard to tear myself away. (*Handing Etienne a certificate*) If your master comes back before I do, give him this. Tell him I examined the customer he sent me, and he's in first rate condition.

ETIENNE. Oh, yes.

FINACHE. Not that you care.

ETIENNE. No. (*He moves to the table* L *and puts the certificate on it*)

FINACHE (*moving down* C) Nor do I. But since your master's the managing director of the Boston Life Insurance Company for Paris and the provinces . . .

ETIENNE. The governor . . .

FINACHE. The governor, if you prefer the word, should know that his Spanish insurance risk is A1. What's he call himself—Don Carlos Homenides de Histangua?

ETIENNE. His wife's here now! She's waiting next door for madame.

FINACHE. Amazingly small world! I examine the husband this morning—and now the wife's next door.

ETIENNE. And they both had dinner here—yesterday!

FINACHE. Unbelievable!

ETIENNE (*sitting* L *of the table*) Doctor. Seeing you're here . . .

FINACHE. You don't stand on ceremony, do you?

ETIENNE. Me? Oh, no. I'm very easy-going. I want to talk to you; because I was having a word the other day with my good lady . . .

FINACHE. Madame Chandebise.

ETIENNE. Not the mistress, my good lady.

FINACHE. Your wife?

ETIENNE. Yes. Now when you've got this hammering inside you —do pull up a chair . . .

FINACHE. Thanks. (*He sits* R *of the table*)

ETIENNE. Night and day. Both sides of the abdomen. Remorseless.

FINACHE (*putting his hat on the table*) Now that's a condition we often find . . .

ETIENNE. Yes?

FINACHE. With some gynaecological troubles.

ETIENNE. I see.

FINACHE. Probably the ovaries.

ETIENNE. That's what I've got?

FINACHE. We'll have to have them out!

ETIENNE. Careful now. (*Rising and moving up* C) If I've got them I'm keeping them.

FINACHE (*also getting up*) I won't insist—on having them. Not for the moment. (*He moves down* L)

(LUCIENNE *enters up* R *and moves up* C)

LUCIENNE. Look here, excuse me. You're sure Madame Chandbise'll be back?

ETIENNE. She said to me, she said, "If Madame—well, anyway . . . whatever your name is.

LUCIENNE. Homenides de Histangua.

ETIENNE. That's right. She told me, "Don't let her go. I've got to see her."

LUCIENNE. That's what she said in her letter. I can't understand it. I'll wait a little longer. (*She moves above the sofa*)

ETIENNE. That's perfectly all right. I was just passing the time of day with the doctor.

FINACHE. He's delightful company.

ETIENNE. That's true. You know Dr Finache?

FINACHE. Madame.

ETIENNE. Chief Medical Officer of the Boston Life.

LUCIENNE. Ah! (*She moves down* C)

ETIENNE. Tells me he saw your husband this very morning.

LUCIENNE. What a coincidence!

FINACHE (*moving to Lucienne* C) I had the honour of examining Don Carlos de Histangua.

(ETIENNE *moves down* L)

LUCIENNE. My husband had himself examined? What on earth for?

FINACHE. Insurance companies are ridiculously inquisitive. But I must congratulate you. What a husband you have, madame! What a constitution! What stamina!

LUCIENNE (*turning away* R) Don't I know it!

FINACHE. It's very flattering.

LUCIENNE. But exhausting!

FINACHE. You get nothing without working for it in this world.

ETIENNE. It's what Madame Plucheux dreams about.

LUCIENNE. Who on earth's that?

ETIENNE. My wife. Too much for me, I can tell you, she needs a man like madame's husband.

FINACHE. Then with madame's permission and the Spanish gentleman's consent—the thing might be arranged!

ETIENNE. God forbid!

LUCIENNE. Really, Doctor! Anyway, I couldn't allow it either.

FINACHE. I'm sorry. (*Picking up his hat from the table*) It's this ghastly butler. He makes me say the most idiotic things. Back in a quarter of an hour. Charming to meet you . . . (*He moves up* C)

ETIENNE (*moving up* C) It's when I lean forward like this they get me.

FINACHE. What?

ETIENNE. Those ovaries!

FINACHE. Oh, take three cascara tablets. That'll give them something to think about.

(FINACHE *and* ETIENNE *exit up* C)

LUCIENNE (*moving to the window* R) Seven minutes past one! (*She picks up a magazine from the table* R) This is what Raymonde calls counting the seconds till she sees me. Really! (*She sits* RC)

(CAMILLE *enters up* L *with a file and moves to the cabinet*)

CAMILLE (*putting the file in the cabinet*) Ho—Hi—Hohiy. (*Oh, I'm sorry*) (*He moves down* C)

LUCIENNE. What did you say?

CAMILLE. Haham's ha—ing hor he hea Hon Hon Hife Cumbee? (*Madame's waiting for the Head of the Boston Life Company?*)

LUCIENNE. I'm terribly sorry . . .

CAMILLE. Haham's ha—ing hor he hea Hon Hon Hife Cumhee?

LUCIENNE (*rising and backing* R) I can't understand a word you're saying.

CAMILLE. He harsed H—Ham here Hee Hee Hirerector? (*I asked if madame's here to see the Director?*)

LUCIENNE (*moving to Camille* C) No. Me. Franzuski—Franchese. Me French.

CAMILLE. He Hoo! (*Me too!*)

LUCIENNE (*backing to the window*) Are you looking for the butler? I mean I don't belong here. I'm just waiting for Madame Chandebise and . . .

CAMILLE (*backing to the door up* L) Ho Horry. (*So sorry*) If madame's waiting for the head of the Boston Life Company.

LUCIENNE. Yes.

CAMILLE. Ho horry. (*So sorry*)

(CAMILLE *exits up* L)

LUCIENNE. What a monster!

(ETIENNE *enters up* C)

ETIENNE. You're not bored?

LUCIENNE (*moving up* C) No, but would you kindly explain—there was a man here . . .

ETIENNE. A man!

LUCIENNE. Spoke the most extraordinary language. Ho Horry H'am . . .

ETIENNE. It's Camille!
LUCIENNE. A foreigner?

(LUCIENNE *and* ETIENNE *move down* C)

ETIENNE. Not at all. The master's nephew. Blood relative. I see your difficulty. He butchers the language. Kills off his consonants entirely.
LUCIENNE. Good heavens!
ETIENNE. It's embarrassing, till you get used to it. I'm just starting to understand . . .
LUCIENNE. He's giving you lessons?
ETIENNE. In time—the ear grows accustomed.
LUCIENNE (*moving* L *below the table*) I suppose it must.
ETIENNE. The master's taken him on as a secretary. Who else would employ him?
LUCIENNE. A man with nothing but vowels to offer!
ETIENNE. It's not enough! He gives you the consonants when he's writing; but we can't all communicate by letter! Such a serious, steady boy. Handicapped! (*Moving* LC) So far as anyone knows, madame, he's never had a woman in his life!
LUCIENNE. Really!
ETIENNE (*simply*) Not so far as we know.
RAYMONDE (*off*) Antoinette, my husband's not back yet—and have you seen Madame de Histangua?
ETIENNE (*moving up* C) Madame's here. (*He opens the door*)
LUCIENNE (*moving up* C) At last!

(RAYMONDE *enters up* C *and kisses Lucienne*)

RAYMONDE. My poor darling—I'm sorry. (*She moves to the stool up* R) You can go, Etienne.
ETIENNE. Yes, madame. Madame will excuse me . . .

(ETIENNE *exits up* C)

LUCIENNE. What's the matter?
RAYMONDE (*taking off her hat*) I've kept you waiting. (*She puts her hat on the stool*)
LUCIENNE. Have you. Really!
RAYMONDE (*moving above the table* LC *and putting her bag on it*) I had to go such a long way. I'll tell you all about it, Lucienne. I wrote and asked you to come because—a terrible thing's happened. My husband's unfaithful.
LUCIENNE. Victor Emmanuel?
RAYMONDE. Exactly! Victor Emmanuel!
LUCIENNE. You take my breath away!
RAYMONDE (*crossing down* R) I'll expose him!
LUCIENNE (*moving down* C) You mean you can prove it?
RAYMONDE. What? Oh, no. I can't. Oh, but I will . . .
LUCIENNE. What?
RAYMONDE. Prove it.
LUCIENNE. How?

RAYMONDE. I don't know. But you're here . . .

LUCIENNE. Well?

RAYMONDE. You're going to prove it for me!

LUCIENNE. Me?

RAYMONDE (*moving* c *and taking Lucienne's hand*) Don't say "no", Lucienne. We were bosom friends at the convent. All right, we've drifted apart over the years, but some things last! I left you Lucienne Vicard. Now I find you Lucienne Homenides de Histangua. The name's longer, but the heart's still in the same place. I always think of you as my best friend. (*She leads Lucienne* R)

LUCIENNE. Of course . . . (*She sits in the chair* RC)

RAYMONDE (*sitting* R *on the sofa*) So I naturally come to you when I have an enormous favour to ask . . .

LUCIENNE. Thank you very much!

RAYMONDE. So tell me what to do!

LUCIENNE. How do you mean?

RAYMONDE. To expose my husband. Trap him . . .

LUCIENNE. Is that why you dragged me here?

RAYMONDE. Well, of course.

LUCIENNE. How do you know he's trappable? He might be a model of virtue.

RAYMONDE. Him!

LUCIENNE. You've got no proof.

RAYMONDE. Certain things, don't deceive you . . .

LUCIENNE. Including Victor Emmanuel?

RAYMONDE. What would you say if *your* husband, suddenly, after having been a husband—and what a husband!—suddenly stopped —like that! Between one day and the next.

LUCIENNE. I'd say—phew!

RAYMONDE. Is that what you'd say? You'd say "phew"? That's what you would say. I was just like you. "This endless love! That perpetual spring. Boring! Tedious! Oh, for a little cloud! A few obstacles. I even thought about taking a lover just for the worry of it.

LUCIENNE. You—a lover!

RAYMONDE. Certainly! You know, you get these moments. Oh, I'd even chosen him. Romain Tournel, to mention no names. He was here with you at dinner the other night. Didn't you notice how he fancied me? You astonish me. Well—we were on the very brink . . .

LUCIENNE. Oh!

RAYMONDE (*rising*) He said, "As your husband's my best friend I feel it's incumbent upon me to . . . Well, why shouldn't I take a lover! Now my Victor Emmanuel's deceiving me! (*She moves* L *and puts her gloves on the table*)

LUCIENNE (*getting up and moving* c) Shall I tell you something?

RAYMONDE. What?

LUCIENNE. You're secretly mad about your Victor Emmanuel.

RAYMONDE. Mad?

LUCIENNE. If you're not—why all the fuss?

RAYMONDE (*moving down* L) Well, I may want to deceive him, but for him to deceive me! No! It's going too far!

LUCIENNE. I like your sense of morality!

RAYMONDE. Aren't I totally justified?

LUCIENNE. Yes, yes. Only look. What you told me doesn't prove anything!

RAYMONDE. What? When a husband's been a raging torrent for years, and then suddenly—pfutt! Nothing. Not a trickle . . .

LUCIENNE (*sitting* R *of the table* LC) Spain's full of dried-up rivers. But they're still in the same old beds . . .

RAYMONDE (*facing front*) Oh . . .

LUCIENNE. You know, it's like those men in casinos, who try to impress everyone by risking millions and then one day—phfft!—they're reduced to ten francs.

RAYMONDE. Ten francs would be all right, but he doesn't even play. All he does is walk round the table and watch.

LUCIENNE. All the better! It doesn't mean he's spending his money on someone else. He's just bankrupt.

RAYMONDE (*moving above the table*) Oh, yes? What about *that*, then? (*She takes a pair of braces from her bag*)

LUCIENNE. What about it?

RAYMONDE. A pair of braces.

LUCIENNE. I can see that.

RAYMONDE. And who do you think they belong to?

LUCIENNE. Your husband, I assume.

RAYMONDE. You admit it!

LUCIENNE. Not exactly. I just presume that if you have a pair of braces about you they belong to your husband, *and no-one else!*

RAYMONDE (*taking her handbag to the stool up* R *and returning down* C) Precisely! And now perhaps you can explain why he got them this morning, through the post.

LUCIENNE. Through the post?

RAYMONDE. In a parcel which I opened by mistake, when I went through his letters.

LUCIENNE. Why go through his letters?

RAYMONDE. To see what's in them.

LUCIENNE. Sound reason . . .

RAYMONDE. Well!

LUCIENNE. That's what you call a parcel "opened by mistake"?

RAYMONDE. Of course it was a mistake. It wasn't meant for me.

LUCIENNE. I see . . .

RAYMONDE. You agree that if someone posts him his braces, it's because he left them behind in some—*somewhere?*

LUCIENNE (*rising and moving down stage*) It seems to follow.

RAYMONDE (*moving* R *of Lucienne*) Yes—and do you know where it was? This "*somewhere*"?

LUCIENNE. You're making my flesh creep.

RAYMONDE. "The Hotel Coq d'Or", my darling.

LUCIENNE. What on earth's that?

RAYMONDE. Well, it's not the Christian Science Reading Room.

LUCIENNE. "The Hotel Coq d'Or."

RAYMONDE (*moving to the tallboy and taking out a box*) Look! The box they came in. Printed label, and then, my husband's address: "Monsieur Chandebise, 95 Boulevard Malesherbes." (*She gives Lucienne the box*)

LUCIENNE. The Hotel Coq d'Or.

RAYMONDE. And in Montretout, my darling. (*She takes the box back*) A name that speaks volumes! It's repulsive! But it adds up! Now I can understand it all. (*She returns the box to the drawer*)

LUCIENNE. Oh? Absolutely.

RAYMONDE (*moving above the sofa*) Of course I had my doubts. Just because my husband seemed to be going through . . . a slight period of . . .

LUCIENNE. Drought?

RAYMONDE. Exactly. I said to myself, "Oh, well," I said. "What of it?" But now—this! This has sent me away—with an enormous flea in my ear . . . (*She moves L of the sofa*)

LUCIENNE. Obviously.

RAYMONDE. If you could see this hotel, darling. It looks as if it'd been carved out of nougat.

LUCIENNE (*moving to L of Raymonde*) You mean, you know it?

RAYMONDE. I've just been there.

LUCIENNE. What?

RAYMONDE. That's why I'm late. I wanted to be quite sure! So I told myself, "You must question the management." But how do you question that type of management? They refused to remember anything.

LUCIENNE. That's the first rule of their profession.

RAYMONDE. You know what the terrible man there said to me?

LUCIENNE. What?

RAYMONDE. He said, "Madame," he said, "if I gave away the names of my guests you'd be the first never to come here any more." He said that to me! Then he shut up. Like a clam. (*She moves down R*)

LUCIENNE. Oh, clam's too good for that sort.

RAYMONDE. You see—men stick together. (*She moves to Lucienne*) We must rely on us! Now—you know so much more about these things than I do, darling.

LUCIENNE (*moving down LC*) I wouldn't say that.

RAYMONDE. You know the facts. And with your touch of genius.

LUCIENNE (*sitting R of the table*) There is that! Of course.

RAYMONDE. What shall I do?

LUCIENNE. Well, now. Let's see. Go to Victor Emmanuel—have it out with him!

RAYMONDE (*moving down C*) Lucienne! You know he'd only lie to me! There's no liar like a man—unless it's a woman.

LUCIENNE (*rising*) You're right. (*Moving to Raymonde*) Men and women are the only two of God's creatures who lie at all. Listen. There's one trick I've seen in plays and . . .

RAYMONDE. What? Tell me.

LUCIENNE. It's pretty loathsome. I mean I'd only do it to a man. But—you take a sheet of highly perfumed writing paper and on it you write a burning, passionate letter . . .

RAYMONDE. Yes?

LUCIENNE. To your husband.

RAYMONDE. Oh . . .

LUCIENNE. As if it came from another woman—and you end up—by arranging a meeting!

RAYMONDE. A meeting?

LUCIENNE. Which you go to, naturally. And if he comes to meet you—you've got him!

RAYMONDE (*bringing the desk from down* R *to the sofa*) Of course. You're right. It's rather revolting, but the old-fashioned ways are best. We'll do it now.

LUCIENNE. Good.

RAYMONDE. He might recognize my handwriting.

LUCIENNE. If you've written to him before.

RAYMONDE. But he doesn't know yours. (*Moving to Lucienne*) You're going to write it! Are you my best friend or not? (*She takes Lucienne's hand*)

LUCIENNE. You're leading me into mortal sin . . .

RAYMONDE. That's where you'll find my husband.

LUCIENNE. That won't do me much good apparently. (*Moving to the sofa*) All right. Give me the writing paper. (*She sits behind the desk*)

RAYMONDE. Here. (*She moves* L *of the desk*)

LUCIENNE. Not yours. He'll recognize it.

RAYMONDE (*moving to the cabinet* R) Of course. Silly of me. This'll do. (*She brings down some paper*) I bought it to give my dear little nephews for their thank you letters.

LUCIENNE. That! He'll think it's an affair with a cook. He'll never go.

RAYMONDE. You're right . . . (*She returns the paper to the cabinet*)

LUCIENNE. Haven't you got any decadent writing paper? Something suggestive . . .

RAYMONDE. There's this mauve. It's not all that suggestive.

LUCIENNE. But drenched in perfume . . .

RAYMONDE (*moving to the bell-push* R *and ringing it*) I've got the stuff! A bottle of "Scarlet Woman". I was going to send it back—it makes me sneeze. Wait a moment.

(CAMILLE *enters up* L)

CAMILLE. Ho Horry. (*So sorry*)

RAYMONDE. Can I help you, Camille?

CAMILLE (*moving down* C) Don't worry. I wanted to see if Victor Emmanuel was back.

RAYMONDE. Not yet. Why?

CAMILLE. There's the post to be signed, and a contract.

RAYMONDE. He can't be much longer.

CAMILLE. I'll wait.

RAYMONDE. All right. What're you staring at, darling?

LUCIENNE. No—nothing, really . . .

CAMILLE. You see Raymonde came home in the end. You didn't have to wait too long.

LUCIENNE. Honestly. I remember you perfectly—we even had a little chat.

RAYMONDE. What he said was—you didn't have to wait too long.

CAMILLE. That's it! That's it!

LUCIENNE. Not too long, thank you.

RAYMONDE. Camille Chandebise, our nephew. Mme Carlos Homenides de Histangua.

LUCIENNE (*rising and offering Camille her hand*) Delighted to meet you. You must excuse me. (*Withdrawing her hand before Camille can kiss it*) I didn't catch all you said just now. A little hard of . . .

CAMILLE. Hearing? I have an impediment—in my speech. I don't say words clearly.

LUCIENNE. Charming! Charming! (*Moving to Raymonde*) What's he talking about?

RAYMONDE. He says he has an impediment in his speech.

LUCIENNE. Really? Well, perhaps a little tiny—hitch. (*Moving down* R) Now you mention it . . .

CAMILLE. You're too kind.

(ANTOINETTE *enters up* C)

ANTOINETTE. You rang, madame.

RAYMONDE. Yes. Fetch me a big bottle of perfume—you'll find it on the right of the dressing-table.

ANTONETTE. Yes, madame.

RAYMONDE. You'll see a "Scarlet Woman" . . . smouldering on the label.

ANTOINETTE. Certainly, madame.

(ANTOINETTE *exits up* R *pinching Camille as she passes*)

CAMILLE. Ouch!

RAYMONDE
LUCIENNE } (*together*) What?

CAMILLE. Touch of neuralgia . . .

RAYMONDE. In the . . .

CAMILLE. Hi' . . .

RAYMONDE. The change in the weather.

CAMILLE. I must get on with my work. (*Moving up* L) Madame.

LUCIENNE. Sir!

CAMILLE. My respects.

(CAMILLE *exits up* L)

LUCIENNE. I think it's wonderful. How do you understand?

RAYMONDE. Is *that* why you were staring?

LUCIENNE. Of course. (*She sits at the desk*)

RAYMONDE. You get used to it. How sweet of you to pretend not to notice . . .

LUCIENNE. I wouldn't hurt his feelings . . .

(ANTOINETTE *enters up* R *to* R *of Raymonde*)

ANTOINETTE. Is this the one, madame?

RAYMONDE. Thank you. Right—now before Victor Emmanuel gets back . . .

(ANTOINETTE *exits up* C)

LUCIENNE. Well, now how are we going to hook the fish?

RAYMONDE. That's the question. (*She sits in the chair* RC)

LUCIENNE. The question is—where?

RAYMONDE. What?

LUCIENNE. Where did this mysterious lady become besotted with Victor Emmanuel?

RAYMONDE. Where do you suggest?

LUCIENNE. Been to the theatre lately?

RAYMONDE. Last Wednesday. The Palais-Royal. We went with Monsieur Tournel . . .

LUCIENNE. Monsieur Tournel?

RAYMONDE. Who's almost my lover . . .

LUCIENNE. Oh, him. (*Writing*) Now—listen to this—"Dear Sir, Having noticed you the other evening at the Palais Royal Theatre . . ."

RAYMONDE. Doesn't that sound a little formal—for love at first sight?

LUCIENNE. Formal?

RAYMONDE. As if you were serving a writ. (*Rising and crossing down* L) I'd come right out with it. "I was the girl who couldn't take her eyes off you that night at the Palais Royal . . ."

LUCIENNE. You've obviously got a talent for this sort of thing.

RAYMONDE. I was only saying what *I'd* write.

LUCIENNE. All right, I agree. "I'm the girl who couldn't take her eyes off you——"

RAYMONDE (*moving* C) "—that night at the Palais Royal." Hot, yearning—and simple.

LUCIENNE. You're really living the part, aren't you? "You were in a box with your wife and another man . . ."

RAYMONDE. Monsieur Tournel . . .

LUCIENNE. "Since then—you are all I dream of."

RAYMONDE (*moving above the sofa to the window*) Isn't that going too far?

LUCIENNE. Other people always go too far.

RAYMONDE. If you're sure . . .

LUCIENNE. "I'm ready to commit a folly. Will you join me? I'll be waiting for you today. Five o'clock. In the Hotel Coq d'Or in Montretout."

RAYMONDE. The same hotel? Won't he be suspicious?

LUCIENNE. He'll be stimulated—beyond endurance. "The room will be booked in the name of Monsieur Chandebise."

RAYMONDE. "I rely on you . . ."

LUCIENNE. "I rely on you." Marvellous! I tell you, you've got a talent for this sort of thing.

RAYMONDE. I'm starting to learn . . .

LUCIENNE (*writing*) "From one who loves you . . ." Now—drenched in perfume . . .

RAYMONDE (*giving Lucienne the perfume*) Here we are!

(LUCIENNE *sprinkles the letter*)

LUCIENNE. That'll do . . . (*She puts the perfume on the table* RC)

RAYMONDE. Oh, dear!

LUCIENNE (*rising*) Blotched!

RAYMONDE. What a shame.

LUCIENNE. Yes.

RAYMONDE. You'll have to do it again.

LUCIENNE (*sitting as before*) Not at all! That'll come in very useful. (*Writing*) "P.S. Why can't I stop crying when I write to you? Let them be tears of joy and not despair." Private. To Monsieur Victor Emmanuel Chandebise. Ninety-five Boulevard Malesherbes. Now we need a messenger. Who can we send?

RAYMONDE. You, of course.

LUCIENNE (*rising*) You're—not serious!

RAYMONDE (*returning the desk to the window*) We can't send a servant —he'd be recognized. And I can't do it myself. I mean if my husband asked for a description of the woman who brought the letter—and got a description of me—the cat would just leap out of the bag! You're the one to do it!

LUCIENNE (*moving* C) Whatever next!

RAYMONDE. Are you my best friend or not?

LUCIENNE. I suppose so. You certainly make the most of it.

(*The doorbell rings*)

RAYMONDE. That must be my husband. (*She opens the door up* R) Hurry up. Out this way. Take the door on the right and you are in the hall.

(LUCIENNE *collects her gloves and exits up* R. RAYMONDE *replaces the cap on the perfume bottle, puts it back on the table, and moves down* R. CHANDEBISE *enters* C, *followed by* ETIENNE)

CHANDEBISE (*giving Etienne his cane*) You say the doctor called?

ETIENNE. Yes, sir.

CHANDEBISE. Good! Excellent! Go in, my dear fellow.

(TOURNEL *enters* C *with a brief-case, which he puts on the table* L)

Give me a moment. Must sign the post. (*He puts his hat and gloves on the table down* L)

(TOURNEL *moves down* L *of the table*)

RAYMONDE. Camille's been waiting as if you were the Second Coming.

CHANDEBISE. Oh, it's you.

TOURNEL. Good morning dear lady.

RAYMONDE. Good morning, Mr Tournel. (*To Chandebise*) Yes, it's me.

CHANDEBISE. I met Tournel on the stairs, so we came up together.

RAYMONDE. Oh, yes . . .

TOURNEL. I've brought a list of new clients.

CHANDEBISE (*hitching up his trousers with his hands in his pockets*) Splei..iid. You can give me that right away.

RAYMONDE. Are you having trouble with your braces by any chance?

CHANDEBISE. As a matter of fact I am.

RAYMONDE. Are they the ones I bought for you?

CHANDEBISE. What's that? Yes, of course.

RAYMONDE. They seemed to be—quite satisfactory.

CHANDEBISE. It's because I've pulled them up too tight.

RAYMONDE (*moving* C) Let me adjust them for you.

CHANDEBISE. Please don't bother. I can adjust them myself.

RAYMONDE. Have it your own way.

CHANDEBISE (*moving up* L) Excuse me. Be with you in a moment.

(CHANDEBISE *exits up* L)

TOURNEL. Carry on! Carry on!

CAMILLE (*off*) A—Harst (*At last*)

CHANDEBISE (*off*) All right! Some people don't have to rush round all day . . . (*He closes the door*)

TOURNEL (*moving* C) Oh, Raymonde! Raymonde! You're all I dream of!

RAYMONDE. Not now, thank you very much. Not when he's unfaithful.

TOURNEL. What?

RAYMONDE (*moving towards the door up* R) That sort of thing's perfectly all right when you've got nothing else on your mind.

TOURNEL (*following her*) But, Raymonde—Raymonde, you said— you let me hope . . .

RAYMONDE. Did I? I suppose I did. But he didn't have his braces then. Now that he's got his braces—good-bye!

(RAYMONDE *exits up* R)

TOURNEL. She's going to be a hard nut to crack! Braces. What's she talking about? Braces!

(CAMILLE *enters up* L)

CAMILLE (*moving up* C) Monsieur Tournel, my uncle is asking for you.

TOURNEL (*smiling*) What?

CAMILLE. My uncle is asking for you.

TOURNEL (*crossing the table* L) Don't talk with your mouth full, old boy, it's rude. (*He picks up his brief-case*)

CAMILLE. Wait. "My uncle is ask-ing for you!"

TOURNEL. My uncle is asking for you! Why not say so!

(TOURNEL *exits up* L)

CAMILLE. What an uncouth fellow! Extraordinary thing! (*Moving* LC) I go to all the trouble of fetching him and he gives me a mouthful of abuse!

(FINACHE *and* ETIENNE *enter up* C)

ETIENNE. The master's back.
FINACHE. Good. (*He moves down* C)
ETIENNE. I'll tell him.

(ETIENNE *exits up* L)

CAMILLE. It's a bit thick! I say to him, most politely. "My uncle is asking for you." He makes me repeat it. I write it down for him, and he has the ice-cold nerve to come back with, "All right, why couldn't you say so?" It's the last time I do a favour for a pig like that!
FINACHE. You rehearsing a dramatic monologue?
CAMILLE. It's you, Doctor! I was just complaining about a certain person who . . .
FINACHE (*moving* RC) Oh, all right. Don't explain. Well, you young scallywag? Been on the tiles lately?
CAMILLE (*moving* C) Oh! Shhh!
FINACHE. Of course. You're supposed to be the virginal young Camille. You've got to keep up your reputation . . .

(FINACHE *and* CAMILLE *circle each other*)

CAMILLE. Please!
FINACHE. Doctors have a way of catching little plaster saints with their trousers down. I must say it's very funny. Everyone thinking that you're so innocent.
CAMILLE. I suppose it is really . . .
FINACHE. Have you taken my advice?
CAMILLE. What?
FINACHE. The Hotel Coq d'Or.
CAMILLE. Please!

(FINACHE *and* CAMILLE *circle again*)

FINACHE. Why? We're alone—between friends. You've been there?
CAMILLE. Yes.
FINACHE. What did I tell you? (*He moves* R)
CAMILLE. Oh! (*He moves* L)
FINACHE. Isn't it? When I want a little—relaxation I never go anywhere else. All right, come down to earth and go and fetch your uncle.
CAMILLE. Yes. Of course. (*He moves up* C)
FINACHE (*moving up* C) While I think of it, I'll give you your infernal machine.
CAMILLE. What infernal machine?
FINACHE. What I promised you. At least you'll sound like a human being.

CAMILLE. You've got it!

FINACHE. Now your trouble is—the roof of your mouth hasn't formed properly. The sounds don't bounce off it. They float up—and they get lost somewhere behind your face.

CAMILLE. That's it.

FINACHE (*producing a box with a false palate in it*) So—I've brought you a sounding board. Isn't it pretty?

CAMILLE. Let's see. (*He takes the box*)

FINACHE. A silver roof to your mouth.

CAMILLE. Oh!

FINACHE. Not everyone can say that.

CAMILLE. I'll be able to speak!

FINACHE. What?

CAMILLE. I'll be able . . . (*He starts to insert the palate*)

FINACHE. Not yet! First soak it in boracic. Who knows where it's been!

CAMILLE. You're right! No, but I said. I shall be able to speak.

FINACHE. Of course you will be able to speak! With a little talent you'll be in the *Comedie Francaise*.

CAMILLE (*moving up* c) Ah! I'll soak it in boracic.

CHANDEBISE (*off*) Camille!

FINACHE. Just a minute. They're calling you.

CAMILLE. Tell them—I'll be back in a minute.

(CAMILLE *exits up* c)

CHANDEBISE (*off*) Camille!

(CHANDEBISE *enters up* L)

FINACHE. He'll be back in a minute. (*He moves down* c)

CHANDEBISE (*moving down* L *of Finache*) Finache!

FINACHE. He's got something to see to. Keeping well?

CHANDEBISE. Thank God it's you—just the man I wanted to see.

FINACHE. I was here earlier. Etienne told you?

CHANDEBISE (*moving below the table to* L *of it*) With Histangua's certificate.

FINACHE. It's on the table.

CHANDEBISE. It seems he's a good risk.

FINACHE. First rate.

CHANDEBISE. Thanks.

FINACHE (*sitting* R *of the table*) What did you want to see me about?

CHANDEBISE (*sitting* L *of the table*) Yes. Well. Now—I wanted to consult you. It's rather a delicate matter. But, quite frankly, a most extraordinary thing's happened to me.

FINACHE. What sort of thing?

CHANDEBISE. It's not very easy to explain. Well. You know I have an extremely attractive wife . . .

FINACHE. Hear, hear!

CHANDEBISE. Good! And no-one's less interested in other women than your humble servant.

FINACHE. Ah.

CHANDEBISE. What do you mean "Ah"? Why do you say "Ah"?

FINACHE. I really don't know.

CHANDEBISE. I'm telling you! Raymonde's everything to me. Wife and mistress. And I don't wish to boast but between you and me, I'm a first-rate husband!

FINACHE. Ah?

CHANDEBISE. What do you mean "Ah"? Why do you keep saying "Ah"?

FINACHE. I really don't know.

CHANDEBISE. I'm telling you! To say I'm first-rate's an understatement . . .

FINACHE. Delighted to hear it. I suppose all this is leading somewhere.

CHANDEBISE. Of course it is. You've seen a play called *Nothing to Declare* at the Palais Royal?

FINACHE. What?

CHANDEBISE. I asked you if you'd seen *Nothing to Declare*.

FINACHE. Yes and no . . .

CHANDEBISE. What's the matter? You've either seen it or you haven't . . .

FINACHE. Well, actually both. I had a close friend in my box.

CHANDEBISE. So there were gaps.

FINACHE. Quite a few.

CHANDEBISE. Never mind! You got the general idea. Nice young man on his honeymoon. He's about to give his wife lesson number one in the grammar of matrimony when a customs officer bursts in with a quite inopportune cry of "Nothing to declare?" Brutally interrupts his train of thought.

FINACHE. I remember, vaguely.

CHANDEBISE. Vaguely! Obviously the customs officer didn't burst into your box!

FINACHE. That's perfectly true.

CHANDEBISE. Not to make a long story out of it—it became an obsession with the young fellow. Every time he felt an impulse to reopen negotiations with madame he saw the customs officer and heard that terrible "Nothing to declare". And then, hey presto! Nothing to declare!

FINACHE. What a bore for him.

CHANDEBISE (*rising and crossing above the table to* C) Decidedly! My dear chap. That's exactly what happens to me!

FINACHE. What?

CHANDEBISE (*pacing down* R *and back to* C) One fine day. No. One ghastly night about a month ago, I was extremely amorous, as is my wont. I expressed my desires to Madame Chandebise who appeared to welcome them. And then, hey presto!

FINACHE. The customs man arrived!

CHANDEBISE. Yes. What? No! But I was in a terrible trouble. I don't know what. I felt I'd become—a little child again.

FINACHE. That was a bit hard.

CHANDEBISE. You could put it more happily. At first—I didn't worry. I had a glorious past behind me. I said to myself, "Chandebise. A reverse today, revenge tomorrow."

FINACHE. That's life!

CHANDEBISE. But the next day unfortunately I said to myself, "Steady now, old fellow. If you're going to do the same as yesterday . . ." Damn silly to put ideas in a man's head just when he needs all his confidence. I was overcome with anxiety and once again. Nothing to declare!

FINACHE. Poor old Chandebise.

CHANDEBISE (*moving* C) I'm afraid it is "poor old Chandebise". It's an obsession. Now I don't even say to myself, "Tonight—can I?" I say, "Tonight—I can't!" It never fails. Steady on! Hardly the moment for laughing.

FINACHE (*rising and moving* C *to Chandebise*) What? You don't expect me to treat your case as a tragedy! It happens every day. You're simply the victim of auto-suggestion. Now! It's up to you. All you need is a little strength of character. If you want it you can do it.

CHANDEBISE (*unconvinced*) Oh, yes!

FINACHE. If instead of saying, "Can I," you must simply say— (*very positive*)—"I can". That'll do it. Never doubt yourself in this life. You should have told your wife all you told me, quite clearly, and calmly . . . I mean, she'd have had a good laugh, and you'd have enjoyed the joke together. You'd've both put your shoulders to the wheel. And rolled straight through the Customs.

CHANDEBISE. Perhaps you're right.

FINACHE. Apart from that I prescribe—plenty of outdoor exercise. I'll listen-in to your chest. You work too hard. Desk-bound. Round shoulders. That's why I prescribed special American braces. I bet you're not wearing them!

CHANDEBISE (*taking off his jacket*) Oh, yes, I am. I gave Camille my other braces. But these are pretty unsightly.

FINACHE. You're the only one who sees them.

CHANDEBISE. It's not true! (*Crossing below the table* L) My wife almost poked her nose in there . . .

FINACHE. That'll never do. (*Following Chandebise*) Come on, let's listen to your chest . . .

CHANDEBISE (*unbuttoning his waistcoat*) One humiliation after another . . .

LUCIENNE (*off* C) Tell your mistress I'm here . . .

CHANDEBISE. Oh! (*He moves down* L *and buttons his waistcoat*)

ETIENNE (*off* C) Certainly, madame.

(LUCIENNE *enters up* C)

CHANDEBISE. See you later. It's you, dear lady . . .

LUCIENNE. Of course it's me. Are you quite well?

CHANDEBISE. Perfectly well, thank you. (*He puts on his jacket*) You're calling on my wife?

LUCIENNE (*moving down* C) Calling back. I had a few—little jobs— but I've seen her already—and this gentleman.

FINACHE. A delightful encounter.

CHANDEBISE. Then—no need for introductions. Did you notice any—signs of nervousness?

LUCIENNE. In him?

CHANDEBISE. No, no. (*Moving* c *to Lucienne*) In my wife. I don't know what was wrong with her this morning. Got out of bed the wrong side . . .

LUCIENNE. I didn't notice anything.

CHANDEBISE. So much the better.

(RAYMONDE *enters* R *and moves above the sofa*)

RAYMONDE. There you are.

LUCIENNE (*moving up to Raymonde*) Hullo again.

RAYMONDE. All right?

LUCIENNE. Fine. It's on its way.

RAYMONDE. Splendid.

(ETIENNE *enters up* c *with the letter*)

ETIENNE. Sir. (*He moves down stage*)

CHANDEBISE. What?

LUCIENNE. Here it is!

ETIENNE. By special delivery. Personal to the master.

(ETIENNE *exits up* C. RAYMONDE *moves down* c)

CHANDEBISE. For me? Excuse me . . . (*He opens the letter*) Good heavens!

RAYMONDE. What is it?

CHANDEBISE. Oh, nothing very much . . .

RAYMONDE. Bad news?

CHANDEBISE. Just something about the business . . .

RAYMONDE. Oh, yes. Liar! (*Moving up* R) Let's go. Now it's perfectly obvious.

(RAYMONDE *and* LUCIENNE *exit* R)

CHANDEBISE (*moving* RC) My dear fellow, women are remarkable creatures! You'll never guess what's happened to me.

FINACHE. What?

(TOURNEL *enters* L *and moves above the table*)

TOURNEL. You gave me the slip . . . (*He puts his case on the table*)

CHANDEBISE. Come in. Nothing private . . .

TOURNEL (*moving down* c) What is it then? Hullo, Doctor.

FINACHE. Oh, hullo, Tournel.

CHANDEBISE. You chaps must amuse yourselves. I've got to go somewhere. I've made a conquest.

TOURNEL } (*together*) What?
FINACHE }

TOURNEL. *You?*

FINACHE. *You*, Chandebise!

CHANDEBISE (*moving between them*) That's taken the wind out of your sails. Listen. And I'm not making this up. "I'm the girl who couldn't take her eyes off you, that night at the Palais Royal . . ."

TOURNEL. *You!*

FINACHE. *You*, Chandebise!

CHANDEBISE. Me! Chandebise! She couldn't take her eyes off me . . .

TOURNEL (*taking the letter and moving* RC) "You were in a box with your wife and another man . . ."

CHANDEBISE. "Another man." That's you, Tournel. (*Taking the letter*) "Another man" "X". The first one she saw, a blurred anonymous individual. Moth-eaten.

TOURNEL. Thank you.

CHANDEBISE. "Since then you're all I dream of."

TOURNEL ⎱ (*together*) No!
FINACHE ⎰

CHANDEBISE. I'm all she dreams of! What've you got to say to that?

TOURNEL. Is that there?

CHANDEBISE. Oh, yes, my dear fellow. It's there all right.

FINACHE. I'm afraid it is.

TOURNEL. Damned odd! Don't you find that damned odd?

FINACHE. People have morbid dreams occasionally.

TOURNEL. Depends on what they ate the night before.

CHANDEBISE. You may choose to mock . . .

TOURNEL. I must say I do . . .

CHANDEBISE (*going on reading*) "I'm ready to commit a folly. Will you join me?" Poor little creature. She's got it badly. Wouldn't you say so?

FINACHE. Oh, I don't know . . .

CHANDEBISE. After what you've heard . . .

FINACHE (*moving below the chair* L *of the table*) Is *that* all?

CHANDEBISE. "I'll be waiting for you today. Five o'clock. At the Hotel Coq d'Or."

FINACHE (*startled*) The Hotel Coq d'Or. (*He sits* L *of the table*)

CHANDEBISE. Yes. In Montretout.

FINACHE. If she knows that place, she must be well broken in.

CHANDEBISE (*moving* R *of the table*) Why? Is it one of those hotels?

FINACHE. It's where I go, for my little adventures.

CHANDEBISE (*sitting* R *of the table*) These places are unknown—to the pure in heart!

FINACHE. But I'm sure Tournel . . .

TOURNEL (*moving* L *above the table*) I may have just heard the name . . .

CHANDEBISE. Oh. My dear fellows . . .

TOURNEL ⎱ (*together*) What?
FINACHE ⎰

CHANDEBISE. She wept!

TOURNEL ⎱ (*together*) No!
FINACHE ⎰

CHANDEBISE. I'm afraid so. Half a minute. "P.S. Why can't I

stop crying when I write to you? Let them be tears of joy and not despair . . ." Poor little broken heart! No good saying she's not totally sincere! Look. Drenched. (*He gives Tournel the letter*)

TOURNEL (*crossing above Chandebrise to* C) Oh, my dear fellows . . .

CHANDEBISE ⎱
FINACHE ⎰ (*together*) What?

TOURNEL. What does she mix her tears with to make them smell so overpowering?

CHANDEBISE (*rising and moving to Tournel*) Did you notice anyone ogling us?

TOURNEL. No! That is—I did notice something. But I thought it was meant for me.

CHANDEBISE (*snatching the letter from Tournel*) Oh. For you? Really. What a fool I am! (*Moving* LC) Of course, it's obvious.

(FINACHE *rises and moves down stage*)

TOURNEL ⎱
FINACHE ⎰ (*together*) What?

CHANDEBISE. It wasn't me she fancied. It was you!

TOURNEL. Me?

CHANDEBISE. Certainly! She mistook you for me. And when someone pointed to our box and said my name, naturally, as she only had eyes for you . . .

TOURNEL. You really think so?

CHANDEBISE. Oh, yes, I'm certain of it.

TOURNEL. Ah. Perhaps so. Yes.

CHANDEBISE. Look at me! Do I sweep girls off their feet? Poor old Chandebise. But you . . . It's perfectly natural. It's your function in life! His function in life. You're used to making conquests. You've the looks.

TOURNEL. Well now. I wouldn't go as far as that . . .

CHANDEBISE. Why not. It's no secret.

FINACHE. You don't know your own strength.

TOURNEL. I may have a certain boyish charm. That's about all . . .

CHANDEBISE. Boyish charm! Women have committed suicide for you. True? Answer yes or no!

TOURNEL. Just—one, actually.

CHANDEBISE. Ah.

TOURNEL. And besides, she recovered.

CHANDEBISE. That's irrelevant!

TOURNEL. Anyway the whole thing's a bit mysterious. She poisoned herself eating mussels.

CHANDEBISE ⎱
FINACHE ⎰ (*together*) *Mussels?*

TOURNEL. I'd just left her. She told everyone she did it in a fit of despair. But I must say I wouldn't choose a plate of *moules marinieres* as a suicide weapon. Too risky.

CHANDEBISE. Come on! There's no mistake. The letter's meant for you.

TOURNEL. What do you think? Doctor?

FINACHE. Well . . .

CHANDEBISE. But of course! And since the letter's meant for you, you're the one who must go . . .

TOURNEL (*moving* R *and twitching his nose*) Oh, I couldn't do that!

CHANDEBISE. Anyway! I'm not free this evening. We've got a dinner for our American director and . . .

TOURNEL. It's impossible.

CHANDEBISE. You're dying to go.

TOURNEL. Am I?

CHANDEBISE (*moving to Tournel*) Look at your nose. It's twitching.

TOURNEL. My God, it is! (*He crosses below Chandebise to* LC) All right. I accept.

CHANDEBISE. Such a tease! Be off with you! (*He moves above Tournel*)

TOURNEL. It suits me. I was looking forward to another little— adventure. It was all arranged. But it'll have to be postponed.

CHANDEBISE. Who with?

TOURNEL (*turning to Chandebise*) With er—I couldn't possibly tell you. (*He crosses* RC)

CHANDEBISE. He couldn't possibly tell me! What a tease you are.

TOURNEL. Your unknown beauty'll do me for the moment.

CHANDEBISE. Take her, with my compliments. (*He moves* C)

TOURNEL. Too kind! So. Let's have the letter.

CHANDEBISE. You don't need it. You've only got to go to that hotel and ask for the room booked in my name. I mean, I don't get letters like that dropped through the post every day of the week. Some day I want my grandchildren—if I manage to produce grand-children—I want them to come across this letter stuffed away in some attic and say, "Grandpa must have been a damned good-looking fellow to excite such a desperate passion." At least I can be good-looking for posterity. Come on, Finache, old man. Come and hear my chest. (*He picks up his hat and gloves and moves down* L)

TOURNEL. What about the signatures . . .

(FINACHES *moves down* L)

CHANDEBISE. I'll be with you in two ticks. We'll go in there, Finache. No-one'll disturb us.

(FINACHE *and* CHANDEBISE *exit* L)

TOURNEL (*moving* C) The Hotel Coq d'Or. Who's this poor girl who's so besotted with me?

(RAYMONDE *enters* R *and moves* L *of the sofa*)

RAYMONDE. Isn't my husband here?

TOURNEL (*moving* L *of Raymonde*) In there with the doctor. Shall I call him?

RAYMONDE. Don't bother him now. Could you say I've gone out with Madame de Histanga and if I'm late he's not to worry. I may dine with a lady friend . . .

TOURNEL. He'll probably be out too.
RAYMONDE. Why?
TOURNEL. He's got a dinner, for his American director.
RAYMONDE. He said *that*, did he? Not that I mind, in the least; but it just isn't true. The dinner's tomorrow! I saw the invitation . . .
TOURNEL (*moving* L) He's made a mistake then. I'll tell him.
RAYMONDE. Don't get excited. He knows exactly what he's doing. An alibi! So he can come creeping home late and say he mixed up the date. He can't fool me . . .
TOURNEL. Why should he tell me fairy stories?
RAYMONDE. You mean he saves them up for me?
TOURNEL. Of course not! You're putting words in my mouth.
RAYMONDE. Very clever! While my husband's unfaithful you know you won't get anywhere with me—so you want me to believe he's pure as the driven . . .
TOURNEL. But he is. I'm speaking the truth!
RAYMONDE. Really! Well, it makes no difference, he still doesn't —oh, good-bye! (*She moves* R)
TOURNEL (*moving* R) Raymonde . . .
RAYMONDE. Lose yourself.

(RAYMONDE *exits* R)

TOURNEL. She told *me*, to lose myself!

(CAMILLE *enters* C *with a glass and a bottle of boracic acid*)

CAMILLE. Hullo, Monsieur Tournel. You in a better temper now?
TOURNEL. You! (*Crossing* L *below Camille*) Lose yourself!

(TOURNEL *exits up* L. CAMILLE *moves above the table* L)

CAMILLE. What an uncouth fellow! (*Putting the boracic in the glass*) Boracic acid—so hard to come by. There! (*He puts the palate in the glass and places it on the mantelpiece*) Soak yourself, my silver roof! Soak yourself clean!

(ETIENNE *enters* C, *followed by* HOMENIDES)

ETIENNE. Monsieur Don Homenides de Histangua.

(ETIENNE *exits*. HOMENIDES *moves down* C)

HOMENIDES. Buenos dias.
CAMILLE (*moving* L *of Homenides*) Monsieur Histangua.
HOMENIDES. Where is Senor Chandebise?
CAMILLE. He'll be with you in a minute. He's with his doctor.
HOMENIDES (*moving* R) I want to see the Senor Chandebise!

(CHANDEBISE *and* FINACHE *enter* L)

CAMILLE. Here they are. (*He moves up* L)
FINACHE. Just take my advice. That's all.
CHANDEBISE. I understand.
HOMENIDES. My old friend. Buenos dias.

CHANDEBISE (*crossing* R) Very well, thank you . . . (*He shakes hands with Homenides*)

HOMENIDES. And the doctor. In fine health?

FINACHE. Naturally. You all right? (*Moving up* C) I've got to rush away.

HOMENIDES. I excuthe . . . (*He puts his hat, gloves and stick on the sofa*)

FINACHE. Good-bye. (*He opens the door up* C)

ALL. Good-bye.

FINACHE. Whoever get's there, good luck at the Hotel Coq d'Or.

(FINACHE *exits* C)

CAMILLE. Silly old fool!

HOMENIDES. Tell me . . . My wife here?

CHANDEBISE. Certainly. With mine.

HOMENIDES. I thought tho.

CHANDEBISE. I'll tell her . . . (*He starts to move up stage*)

HOMENIDES (*crossing* L *below the table*) Chandebise, I called on your company today. I thaw your doctor.

CHANDEBISE. He told me.

HOMENIDES. He told me—"Per favor to make a little water".

CHANDEBISE (*moving down* C) What?

HOMENIDES. Pee—piddle—*pith!*

CHANDEBISE. Ah yes!

HOMENIDES. Why did he do that?

CHANDEBISE. What?

HOMENIDES. To make me—pith?

CHANDEBISE. Well obviously—to discover if you're a good risk.

HOMENIDES. But I came to insure my wife!

CHANDEBISE. You should've told me.

HOMENIDES. I thaid I want inthurance. You didn't ask me for who.

CHANDEBISE. Well, no harm done. Your wife can just pop into the company office and . . .

HOMENIDES. Be subjected—to the same humiliation?

CHANDEBISE. Well, of course.

HOMENIDES. I'm not wanting that.

CHANDEBISE. But . . .

HOMENIDES (*moving slowly* C) I'm not wanting *that!* I'm not wanting *that!* I am not wanting that!

CHANDEBISE. Now. Be reasonable. It's in our rules.

HOMENIDES. I break your rules. I have already pithed for her.

CHANDEBISE. That's not allowed.

HOMENIDES (*moving* LC) Bueno. Then no inthurance. Terminado!

CHANDEBISE. Surely you're not so possessive . . .

HOMENIDES. An affront—to the man of dignity.

CHANDEBISE. Or jealous.

HOMENIDES. Jealouth? Me? I am never jealouth.

CHANDEBISE. Of course you have no reason to be jealous of your wife. I'm sure of that.

HOMENIDES. Not only that! She knows that I would be terrible. She wouldn't dare detheive me . . .

CHANDEBISE. Oh, yes?

HOMENIDES (*producing a revolver*) You thee thith little toy?

CHANDEBISE. Put it away! (*Crossing below Homenides to L of the table*) Good heavens—don't play with things like that!

HOMENIDES (*moving C*) Not dangerous. Just a deterrent.

CHANDEBISE. All the same.

HOMENIDES. If I just cath her—with another man. He'll get a ball of shot in the back which will pass through and come *out of the back!*

CHANDEBISE. Out of—his back?

HOMENIDES. No! Hers!

CHANDEBISE. What? Oh, I see. You think they might possibly be like—well, like . . .

HOMENIDES. I think? What do you mean I think?

CHANDEBISE. Nothing. Really, nothing at all.

HOMENIDES. She knows what'll happen. I told her. (*Moving L of the sofa*) On the wedding night . . .

CHANDEBISE (*moving to C*) Charming for her!

(TOURNEL *enters up* L)

TOURNEL. Oh, there you are, old chap. (*He moves down LC*)

CHANDEBISE. Half a moment.

TOURNEL. No, listen. You know I've got—an urgent appointment.

CHANDEBISE. Of course. Get the forms out. (*Moving R to Homenides*) I'll be with you in a second.

TOURNEL. Oy . . . !

(TOURNEL *exits up* L)

HOMENIDES. Who's that man?

CHANDEBISE. Monsieur Tournel.

HOMENIDES. Monsieur Tournel?

CHANDEBISE. One of our agents—and a personal friend.

HOMENIDES. Aha?

CHANDEBISE. Charming fellow. Tournel do meet . . . Oh. He's not there. Pity. He's only got one fault . . .

HOMENIDES. Yes?

CHANDEBISE. Women! He never stops. It's quite fantastic.

HOMENIDES. Well . . .

CHANDEBISE. He's in a hurry. He's got a girl waiting for him now. Or perhaps she's not waiting for him either. You see, she sent her steaming little love letter—to me!

HOMENIDES. Truly? Who is thith girl?

CHANDEBISE. A mystery. Not signed.

HOMENIDES. Perhaps—one of those anonymous perthons.

CHANDEBISE. But she must be a woman of the world. Sophisticated. Married probably.

HOMENIDES. Why you thay this?

CHANDEBISE. What?

HOMENIDES. Why you thay this?

CHANDEBISE. Oh. Why I thay this? Well, the way it's written. Loose women are much more straightforward, not so sentimental. Here, have a look . . . (*He holds out the letter*)
HOMENIDES (*taking the letter and moving down* R) Good joke! A poor idiot of a husband! Being cheated!
CHANDEBISE. That makes you laugh?
HOMENIDES. Such a good joke! (*He looks at the letter*)
CHANDEBISE. He's got a lovely nature!
HOMENIDES. Ah!
CHANDEBISE (*backing* LC) What?
HOMENIDES (*moving up* R, *above the sofa*) Caramba! The moment of truth! Caramba!
CHANDEBISE. What's the matter?
HOMENIDES (*moving* L *of the sofa*) Her handwriting! (*He produces the revolver*)
CHANDEBISE. *What?*
HOMENIDES (*seizing Chandebise and bending him over the table* LC) Mongrel! Snake! Reptile!
CHANDEBISE. There—there, old fellow.
HOMENIDES. My faithful bulldog! Here, boy, here!
CHANDEBISE. He's got a dog with him?
HOMENIDES. There you are!
CHANDEBISE. Steady now . . .
HOMENIDES. My wife thends you letters!
CHANDEBISE (*escaping and running* L *of the table*) Certainly not! Anyway how do you know it's her? These days all women write alike . . .
HOMENIDES (*turning* C *and loading the revolver*) I know it!
CHANDEBISE. Anyway I'm not going to see her. It's Tournel.
HOMENIDES. The man who wath here! Good! I shall kill him!
CHANDEBISE (*moving up* L) I'll stop him going. It'll be all right . . .
HOMENIDES (*stopping him*) I wish it consummated. Then I have my proof—and I will kill beautifully!
LUCIENNE (*off* R) Raymonde, dear, we really ought to hurry.
RAYMONDE (*off* R) Yes, dear, I'm ready.
HOMENIDES. My wife's voice! (*Forcing Chandebise down* L) Get in there . . .   .
CHANDEBISE. Histangua, my dear friend . . .
HOMENIDES. Si! I'm your friend! But I'll kill you like a mongrel dog. Go on. Or I fire.
CHANDEBISE. No—no . . .

(CHANDEBISE *exits down* L. HOMENIDES *locks the door and pockets the letter and revolver*)
(LUCIENNE *and* RAYMONDE *enter up* R. LUCIENNE *moves down* R, RAYMONDE *down* C)

LUCIENNE. Darling, here you are!
HOMENIDES (*moving below the table*) Si! Here I am.
RAYMONDE. Monsieur de Histangua.
HOMENIDES. Madame, I trust you are well. And your huthband . . .

RAYMONDE. Well, yes, thank you very much.

HOMENIDES. And los ninos—the little ones.

RAYMONDE. Well, I haven't any little ones.

HOMENIDES. Pity. Well—thooner or later . . .

RAYMONDE. Thank you.

LUCIENNE. What's the matter?

HOMENIDES. Nothing the matter. Nothing! Nada . . .

LUCIENNE. I'm going out with Raymonde. You don't mind?

HOMENIDES. Bueno. Go. I beg you. Go!

LUCIENNE (*moving up* C) Good-bye, then.

RAYMONDE. Good-bye, dear M. de Histangua. (*She moves up* C *and opens the door*)

HOMENIDES. Adios, madame. Good-bye.

LUCIENNE (*moving down* RC) Que tienes, querido mio? Que te pasa por que me pones una cara asi? (*What has happened to you, darling? Why do you make that face?*)

HOMENIDES. Te aseguro que no tengo nada! (*I can assure you nothing has happened to me!*)

LUCIENNE. What an impossible creature!

(RAYMONDE *and* LUCIENNE *exit up* C)

HOMENIDES (*moving down* L) She rejects me! Without thame! (*Moving up* L) Thore! Thrumpet!

(*Knocking is heard off down* L)

(*Moving down* L) Thut up—or I fire!

(TOURNEL *enters up* L *and moves above the table*)

TOURNEL. Isn't Chandebise in here?

HOMENIDES. The other man! Tournel! (*Moving up to Tournel*) No, Senor. He is not here.

TOURNEL. All right, if you see him be so good as to tell him I've left all the proposal forms in his office. He's only got to sign them.

HOMENIDES. Bueno! Bueno!

TOURNEL (*moving up* C) I simply can't wait any longer.

HOMENIDES (*following him*) Go! Go on! Go! Go—or I'll . . .

TOURNEL. Or you'll what?

HOMENIDES. Nada, Senor. Absolutely nada! (*Moving above the table*) Go then. You'd better go.

TOURNEL. All right. Curious individual. Good day.

(TOURNEL *exits up* C)

Ah—I'm choking. I need a drink. (*He drinks from the glass on the mantelpiece*) Filthy French drink! (*He puts the glass on the table and moves down* L)

(CAMILLE *enters up* L *and moves down* C)

CAMILLE. Monsieur Histangua. All alone? (*He offers his hand*)

HOMENIDES (*grabbing him by the throat and swinging him down* L) You . . . ! Oh, you. So happy you're here. I'm going now.

CAMILLE. Oh, yes!

Act I   A FLEA IN HER EAR   27

HOMENIDES. When I go I authorize you—to unlock your mathter.
CAMILLE. My mathter?
HOMENIDES (*collecting his stick, gloves and hat from the sofa*) Oh,
thameless! Lustful! Lecher! Who would think my mujer would think
to a lover!

(HOMENIDES *exits* C)

CAMILLE. My mujer think to a lover! You can't understand a
word he says. My mathter? What mathter? (*He unlocks the door* L)
You . . . ?

(CHANDEBISE *enters down* L)

CHANDEBISE (*in the doorway*) Has he gone?
CAMILLE. Who?
CHANDEBISE. Ho—Homenides.
CAMILLE. Yes.
CHANDEBISE. And—his wife?
CAMILLE. She went out with Raymonde.
CHANDEBISE. Good. And Tournel?
CAMILLE. He's just left.
CHANDEBISE (*crossing below Camille to* C) Him, too. How terrible.
There's not a moment to lose. Who can we send down there to stop
them, I know—Etienne. (*He moves up* C)
CAMILLE (*moving up* C) What's "down there"?
CHANDEBISE. Down there's the—*Place*. The what-do-you-call-it?
—"down there". Good God, we're sitting on a volcano. We're about
to witness a ghastly tragedy. Perhaps—a double murder!
CAMILLE. What are you talking about?
CHANDEBISE. Look. (*Swinging Camille to* R *of him and moving* LC)
I've got time to run round to Tournel's before the dinner. My hat!
Where's my hat?
CAMILLE. What on earth's happening?
CHANDEBISE. No time to explain. If Tournel comes back—tell him
not to go. He knows where. His life's at stake.
CAMILLE. His life's at stake?
CHANDEBISE. Understand? (*Moving down* L) His life's at . . .
CAMILLE. Yes, yes. Stake.
CHANDEBISE. What dramas! Oh, my God! What dramas!

(CHANDEBISE *exits down* L)

CAMILLE (*moving down* R) I feel it in my bones—something's going
on.

(TOURNEL *enters* C)

TOURNEL. I left my brief-case . . . (*He moves to the table* L)
CAMILLE (*crossing to* R *of Tournel*) Monsieur Tournel!
TOURNEL. Here it is. (*He picks up his case*)
CAMILLE. For God's sake. Don't go you know where. Your life's
at stake!
TOURNEL. What did you say?

CAMILLE (*pushing Tournel round to the door up* c) Don't go you know where. Your life's at stake.

TOURNEL. Let me alone! I can't understand a word you say. (*He moves to the door up* c)

CAMILLE (*moving up stage*) Monsieur Tournel! Monsieur Tournel!

TOURNEL. To hell with you! Good-bye!

(TOURNEL *exits up* c, *slamming the door*)

CAMILLE (*moving to the mantelpiece*) My roof. Oh, dear God! My silver roof . . . (*Seeing the glass on the table*) There you are! (*He puts the palate in his mouth and speaks normally*) Monsieur Tournel! (*Moving up* c) Monsieur Tournel!

(CHANDEBISE *enters down* L)

CHANDEBISE (*moving below the table*) Who are you yelling at?

CAMILLE (*moving down* c; *speaking clearly*) At Monsieur Tournel. I've never known such an uncouth fellow! I gave him your message perfectly clearly. He simply wouldn't listen.

CHANDEBISE. My God! He spoke!

CAMILLE (*running up* c) Monsieur Tournel! Monsieur Tournel! Listen to me, Monsieur Tournel!

CAMILLE *exits up* c, *leaving the doors open, as the lights Black-Out and*

the CURTAIN *falls*

ACT II

SCENE—*The Hotel Coq d'Or in Montretout. Evening.*
A staircase to L of C leads to a landing and the upper rooms. Below this is a passage leading off up C. Another corridor up L leads to other rooms in the hotel, and a door down L to Schwarz's bedroom. The R side of the stage is taken up by a small bedroom, the door to which is down stage in the dividing wall. A door down R in the bedroom leads to a bathroom. The bed is on a low rostrum RC, and is on a revolve. When this is turned, a similar bed is moved on from a second room which is up stage of the first. The door to this second room is above the other door in the dividing wall.

When the CURTAIN *rises,* EUGÉNIE *is discovered standing on the chair down R, cleaning the door.* FERAILLON *enters up L, crossing to the bedroom door.*

FERAILLON. Eugénie! (*He enters the bedroom*) Eugénie!

EUGÉNIE. Yes, sir?

FERAILLON. What are you doing?

EUGÉNIE. I'm finishing the room, sir.

FERAILLON. You call this room done, do you?

EUGÉNIE (*getting off the chair*) Looks all right to me. (*She replaces the chair down R*)

FERAILLON. Do you call this a made bed? It looks as if it's been used once or twice since this morning.

EUGÉNIE. Fancy that!

FERAILLON. Are you implying that there's something dubious about this hotel.

EUGÉNIE. Oh, I'd never say that!

(OLYMPE *enters from the corridor C with linen and moves down LC*)

FERAILLON. I tell you this is a respectable establishment! Only married couples come here.

EUGÉNIE. But not at the same time!

(OLYMPE *puts the linen on the table down L and looks in the mirror*)

FERAILLON. Mind your own business. If they're both married, it is twice as respectable. Now let's get this bed straightened.

EUGÉNIE. Oh, for heaven's sake!

FERAILLON. It's a matter of urgency! (*He moves to the stairs*)

EUGÉNIE. He gets on your nerves. (*She tidies the bed*)

OLYMPE. What are you on about, Feraillon.

FERAILLON. That girl needs a sharp lesson. If I'd had her under me in the regiment, I'd have made her jump about a bit.

(EUGÉNIE *exits R*)

OLYMPE. Now then, Feraillon.

(BAPTISTIN *enters from the corridor* C *and tiptoes to the bedroom up* C)

FERAILLON. Oh, I'd have made her double up, about turn. I'm not making any innuendoes.

OLYMPE. I should hope not!

FERAILLON. I can't stand that type of conversation. (*He swings Baptistin down* L, *to* R *of Olympe*) Where've you sprung from? Some filthy bar, I suppose . . .

BAPTISTIN. Me?

FERAILLON. It's five o'clock. On sentry go! (*Crossing below Baptistin to* L *of him*) Do you want to work or not?

BAPTISTIN. Yes.

FERAILLON. All right. Go to bed! (*Seizing Baptistin by the collar*) Here's a perfectly useless individual, offered a golden opportunity to be bedridden with the rheumatics, and I pay him for it! Why? Because I've got too much family feeling to leave an old uncle of mine in the gutter. And how does he repay me? By creeping out in the afternoons. By hanging round the bars . . .

BAPTISTIN. Listen.

FERAILLON. Filthy, depraved, drinking dens which should be closed in the name of public morality. And if we needed a ghastly old wreck in your absence, who'd have taken your place, you ghastly old wreck? Not me, I do assure you! What would we do in a sudden emergency? Who'd have saved us from a nasty case of *in flagrante?*

BAPTISTIN. But I knew . . .

FERAILLON. Silence on parade! And go to your room. To bed!

(BAPTISTIN *exits up* C)

My family's doing all right. All take and no give . . .

(SCHWARZ *enters down* L *and moves to Feraillon*)

SCHWARZ. Hat ein schönes, kleines Mädchen nach mir gefragt?

FERAILLON. What!

SCHWARZ (*turning and moving* R *of Olympe*) Hat ein schönes, kleines Mädchen nach mir gefragt?

OLYMPE. Gefragt? No gefragt at all.

(SCHWARZ *exits down* L)

FERAILLON (*moving down* C) What did he say?

OLYMPE. I have a feeling he's looking for someone.

FERAILLON. It's morbid. Chattering away in Prussian! I don't talk like that to him.

OLYMPE. He doesn't know our language.

FERAILLON. That's no excuse! I don't know his.

(EUGÉNIE *enters* R *with a jug, and moves* C)

OLYMPE. Poor fellow. He's come here three times and every time he's been let down.

FERAILLON. If he behaves like that with women I can understand it.

OLYMPE. There you are, then! (*Picking up the linen*) I'll pop these up in the linen cupboard.
FERAILLON. Let the girl do that, Eugénie!
EUGÉNIE. Yes?
FERAILLON. Is the bedroom done?
EUGÉNIE (*moving below the stairs*) Oh, yes, sir.
FERAILLON (*moving R of the stairs*) It's always done when you want it done.
EUGÉNIE. And when it's done it's always ready to be done again.
FERAILLON. Quite enough of your philosophy. There's a pile of sheets! Take them up to the linen cupboard.
EUGÉNIE. Me?
FERAILLON. Who else?

(EUGÉNIE *moves L and takes the linen*)

EUGÉNIE. Donkey work! (*She starts up the stairs*)
OLYMPE. While I think of it. Don't let that room. It's reserved specially.
FERAILLON (*moving down C*) Who for? (*He sits on the stool and lights a cigar*)
OLYMPE. Monsieur Chandebise. (*Taking a telegram from her garter and moving C*) You remember him?
EUGÉNIE. Oh, yes. The gentlemen that Halked Hike Hat?
OLYMPE. That's him.

(EUGÉNIE *moves down C and looks over Olympe's L shoulder*)

FERAILLON. He's coming today.
OLYMPE. Yes. Here's his telegram. All right, Eugénie.
EUGÉNIE. Oh, yes, madame. Thanks for asking.
OLYMPE. I mean. All right! That will be all . . .
EUGÉNIE. Oh, yes. Sorry (*Facing front*) How very embarrassing! (*She moves up C*)
OLYMPE. Go up the back stairs. Then you won't bump into our clients with your pile of sheets.
EUGÉNIE. Yes, madame.

(EUGÉNIE *exits upstairs*)

OLYMPE. Here's what the telegram says—"Keep me same room as last time. Five o'clock. Signed Chandebise." This is the one he had last time.
FERAILLON (*rising*) That's all right. (*Entering the downstage bedroom*) I'll just inspect the quarters. That's better.
OLYMPE (*following him*) What about the bathroom? The bathroom's vital!

(OLYMPE *exits R*)

FERAILLON. And our camouflage system! Make sure my old idiot uncle's on duty. (*He presses a button L of the bed*)

(*The bed revolves, revealing* BAPTISTIN *in the upstage one*)

BAPTISTIN. My rheumatism. I'm a martyr to it. Can't move hand or foot . . .

FERAILLON. Not now, you fool! It's only me!

BAPTISTIN. You! You're always on at me; but here I am. Manning my post.

FERAILLON (*pressing the button*) That's what I pay you for.

(*The bed revolves.* OLYMPE *enters* R)

(*As the bed turns; to Baptistin*) We'll file you away for future reference. All present and correct. (*Moving below the stairs*) Where's Poche?

OLYMPE (*following to* C) In the cellar, getting the wood up.

FERAILLON. In the cellar? Poche? Are you out of your mind, woman? You know his one weakness, and you send him down to the cellar.

OLYMPE. The wine's locked up. He's quite safe.

FERAILLON. If you knew the old beggar! It's no good him saying he's broken himself of the habit. I know him of old. Had him under me in the regiment. Good as gold Monday to Saturday—but straight after Church Parade, the Sunday morning piss up!

OLYMPE (*moving* R *of Feraillon*) It's fashionable—on Sundays.

FERAILLON. He started the fashion. Did I put him on a charge? Oh, no. I preferred to give him a beautiful hiding which kept him straight till the following Saturday. Then, on Sunday, he'd start all over again. Apart from that he was a credit to the Service, honest, hard-working . . . and, thank God, loyal! Oh, I could chase that one! It was a real pleasure to knock him about. Whenever I got my boot to him, he was a perfect gentleman.

OLYMPE (*putting her hand over his shoulder*) You give such beautiful beatings . . .

FERALLION. Well, yes. I had a certain talent, in that direction. (*Moving* LC) I'm getting past it now. But he's the sort of servant I like. Not this modern type of domestic you have to go down on your knees and beg them to do you a favour. When I discovered Poche had drunk himself out of the army and was selling matches up the Champs Elysées, I gave him a job at once!

OLYMPE. You're a good boy.

(POCHE *enters by the corridor* C, *and salutes*)

FERAILLON. Talk of the devil! What was it, Poche?

POCHE (*holding out a telegram*) Dispatches from the front, chief.

FERAILLON (*crossing below Olympe and taking the telegram*) Dispatches from the front! Right! Thanks. My God, you're an ugly-looking brute these days, Poche. You finished staring at me, half-wit? Chandebise again. (*Reading*) "Keep me a good room . . ."

(EUGÉNIE *enters downstairs and moves* L *of Poche*)

OLYMPE. He's got one!

FERAILLON. "And show anyone in who asks for it in my name." Got it, you pair of . . . ? If anyone asks for the room reserved for Chandebise, show them in there!

EUGÉNIE. All right.
POCHE. Orders received and understood, chief!
FERAILLON. To your posts!

(EUGÉNIE *exits up* L. POCHE *stand still*)

(*Catching Poche by the* L *arm and swinging him round to face the stairs*) Are you deaf, you stinking Cossack? Pa-rade dis—miss! Happy as a babe unborn. He loves me! Wake up—get moving! (*He kicks Poche*)

(POCHE *moves up two stairs*)

By the right! Hipe—hipe!

(POCHE *exits upstairs*)

OLYMPE. He's harmless, anyway.

(SCHWARZ *enters down* L *and crosses above Feraillon to* R *of him*)

SCHWARZ. Entschuldigen Sie mich, bitte, ein Fraülein, ist ein hübsches, junges Fraülein für mich gekommen?
FERAILLON. What!
SCHWARZ (*crossing below Feraillon to* L *of him*) Ein hübsches, junges Fraülein—für mich?
FERAILLON. No, I don't think so.
SCHWARZ (*moving down* L *to the door*) Donnerwetter nocheinmal— (*turning in the doorway*)—danke schön.

(SCHWARZ *exits down* L)

OLYMPE. The demon lover!
FERAILLON. Damn jack in the box.
OLYMPE. Makes you jump out of your skin.
(FINACHE *enters by the corridor* C)
FINACHE. Good afternoon, Colonel.
FERAILLON ⎱ (*together*) ⎰ Hullo, Doctor.
OLYMPE ⎰   ⎱ Afternoon, Doctor.
FINACHE (*moving to Olympe and kissing her hand*) My dear Madame Feraillon. Have you got a room for me?

(FERAILLON *moves down* C)

OLYMPE. Always one for *you*, Doctor.
FINACHE. No-one's—asked for me?
FERAILLON. Not yet, Doctor.
FINACHE. Just as well . . .
OLYMPE. We haven't seen you for more than a month.
FINACHE. I've been flitting from flower to flower.
FERAILLON. That's no good. You must be faithful.
FINACHE. But not always to the same girl.
FERAILLON. I mean faithful to us . . .
FINACHE. That's better.
FERAILLON. If you were faithful in love—we'd be out of business.
FINACHE. How true. (*Moving up stage and back*) Coming in here—it's like going into an enchanted forest! I didn't see your man at the desk.

OLYMPE. Poche?

FINACHE. What, Poche? No, Gabriel.

FERAILLON. You didn't know? It's been so long! He was dismissed the service!

FINACHE. Oh, why? He was so decorative . . .

FERAILLON (*moving close to Finache*) Too damned decorative.

OLYMPE (*moving close to Finache*) He started having affairs with the clients.

FINACHE. You don't say . . .

FERAILLON. We can't have that. A man's got to feel safe to bring his mistress here without having her snaffled by the uniformed staff. We've got our reputation . . .

FINACHE (*moving* R *to the stool down* C) Of course you have.

FERAILLON. You must have discipline! Speaking as an old soldier . . .

FINACHE. So he's a genuine colonel. (*He sits*)

OLYMPE. Perfectly genuine!

FERAILLON. Ex-Regimental Sergeant-Major Feraillon of the Twenty-ninth Foot. That's why they call me colonel.

FINACHE. In civil life . . .

FERAILLON. Oh, in civil life what's a rank or two, here or there? What do you think, my dear? Number Ten for the doctor?

OLYMPE. Yes . . . (*She moves to the stairs*)

FINACHE (*rising*) Isn't Number Five free?

FERAILLON. Afraid not.

(OLYMPE *goes up the stairs*)

FINACHE. Oh, dear . . .

FERAILLON. Number Ten has all the same—facilities.

FINACHE. Number Ten'll have to do.

OLYMPE. I'll get it ready for you.

FERAILLON (*turning and blowing kisses to Olympe*) You do that, my little angel.

(OLYMPE *returns the kisses, and exits*)

FINACHE. What a perfect gem she is!

FERAILLON. A very genuine type of woman.

FINACHE (*moving* C) I often feel—I've seen her before.

FERAILLON. Oh, yes. Didn't you ever hear of the beautiful Castana? Her they used to call "The Copper-Bottomed Contessa"?

FINACHE. The name's familiar . . .

FERAILLON. She was the Duc de Choisel's mistress—for many years.

FINACHE. Wasn't there a Freemason's dinner, where she was served up stark naked with the peche melba? On a silver plate—with sponge fingers!

FERAILLON. You've hit it! That's her. That's my wife! I married her

FINACHE. Congratulations!

FERAILLON. She fell for me when I was a sergeant of the Twenty-ninth. I was a handsome young fellow. Anyway, she always relished something in uniform.

FINACHE. The Copper Bottomed—of course!

FERAILLON. That's it! She—she wanted me to live off her . . .

FINACHE. Really?

FERAILLON. I didn't fancy it. Well, she had a bit in the bank, and her powerful attractions, and her reputation of course. I tell you. She was a catch! So, I proposed marriage, and we worked it out that way.

FINACHE (*moving to the stool down* C) Good for you! (*He sits*)

FERAILLON. I made my position quite clear. From now on, I said, orgies are out! And no more gentlemen. (*Moving* C) I don't know about you, but when I take a wife, gentlemen are definitely out of the question.

FINACHE. I think you're perfectly right.

FERAILLON (*moving* LC) Respectability! I told her, from now on. So we opened up this little business.

FINACHE (*rising*) You're a wise man!

FERAILLON. We live pretty modestly. Putting by for our old age. I was thinking about what you mentioned the other day, life insurance!

FINACHE (*moving* C) You're coming round to it.

FERAILLON. I'm forty-four now, and Madame Feraillon's fifty-two, give or take a little.

FINACHE. Good! They say there should be seven or eight years between a husband and wife . . .

FERAILLON. It might be better if the wife was younger . . .

FINACHE. If there's no alternative, it's got to be the husband.

FERAILLON. Obviously! Now if I can insure my poor darling, so that when she passes away . . .

FINACHE. Insure her! At fifty-two. You'd be much cheaper.

FERAILLON. I don't care which. Just so long as when *she* dies . . .

FINACHE. No! It'd be when *you* die . . .

FERAILLON. When I die? Oh, I'm not thinking of myself it's *her* I'm worried about . . .

FINACHE. We'll work something out. Come and see us.

FERAILLON. When?

(OLYMPE *enters downstairs to the landing*)

FINACHE. Any morning. I'm there from ten to eleven. The French branch of the Boston Life Assurance Company. Ninety-five Boulevard Malesherbes . . .

FERAILLON. Boulevard Malesherbes. Who do I ask for?

FINACHE. Our managing director. I'll warn him.

FERAILLON. Very kind of you.

OLYMPE. Would you like to see the room, Doctor?

FINACHE (*going upstairs*) Of course I'd like to see it. I'm longing to see it! Let me know as soon as anyone asks for me.

(FINACHE *exits upstairs.* OLYMPE *follows*)

FERAILLON. Love! It's a beautiful thing!

(Schwarz *enters down* L)

Schwarz. Haben Sie ein schönes Fräulein für mich?
Feraillon. Stop doing that!
Schwarz. Ein hübsches, kleines Mädchen?
Feraillon. Shut your hole!
Schwarz. Bitte?
Feraillon. Shut your hole!
Schwarz. Schart—ja—hohl?
Feraillon (*moving* L *to Scharz*) That's right—I have the honour to request you to shut your hole.

(Raymonde *enters* c. *She is veiled*)

Schwarz (*shaking Feraillon's hand*) Ach so! Jawohl! Schart ja hohl!

(Raymonde *moves down stage*)

Feraillon. It's a pleasure.
Schwarz (*seeing Raymonde*) Ach! Freude!
Feraillon. At your service, madame.
Raymonde. You have a room booked for Monsieur Chandebise?
Feraillon. This way, madame. (*He goes to the bedroom down* R)

(Raymonde *starts to follow, but is stopped* c *by* Schwarz, *who dances round her, from below, to* R, *then above and to* L *of her, singing*)

Schwarz. Eins, zwei, drei, vier, funf, sechs, sieben, acht,
　　　　　Neun, zehn, elf, zuölf,
　　　　　Ich werde auf dich warten!

(Schwarz *dances off* L)

Raymonde (*shaken*) Insane?
Feraillon (*returning to* R *of Raymonde*) No, madame. Merely Prussian. Here for the Exhibition.
Raymonde (*moving down* L) Exhibition, cheeky fellow! (*Taking off her veil*) No-one's asked for the room yet?
Feraillon. No. No-one. Bless my soul. Aren't you the lady who called this morning. If I'm not very much mistaken.
Raymonde. What?
Feraillon. I knew my tact and discretion would impress you, madame. Testing us out, were you? I thought you planned to bring a customer, but not so soon.
Raymonde. Please! Don't imagine that . . .
Feraillon (*moving to the bedroom door and opening it*) Say no more. If madame would be so good.

(Raymonde *enters the bedroom*. Feraillon *follows*)

Raymonde. Huh!
Feraillon. It's our most comfortable room, madame. (*Moving to the bed*) The bed . . .
Raymonde (*moving down* c) I don't want anything to do with the bed!

FERAILLON. Oh, well! Pervert! (*He opens the door* R) Here's the bathroom, complete with hot and cold, bath, bidet, shower . . .
RAYMONDE. Thank you. I have no intention of moving in.
FERAILLON. Well! Now there's this little convenience I'd like to show madame. Comes in very useful in a sudden case of *in flagrante*. On each side of the bed madame will find a button . . .
RAYMONDE (*moving down* R) I can see it for myself. Please leave me alone.
FERAILLON. But, madame . . .
RAYMONDE. I don't need you any more . . .
FERAILLON (*moving to the bedroom door*) Well—all right then. Always at your service. (*He bows and enters the room* L)
RAYMONDE. Good-bye! Tactless fellow!

(RAYMONDE *exits* R)

FERAILLON. Stuck-up bitch! Poche!

(POCHE *enters downstairs with a log basket*)

POCHE. Yes, Chief!
FERAILLON. Finished lugging the logs?
POCHE. Report for orders, Chief!
FERAILLON (*moving down* L) Get your uniform on. This isn't the place for it. It's time for the customers to arrive. On parade!

(*Number 4 rings on the buzzer board*)

POCHE. Yes, chief.
FERAILLON (*moving to the board*) Someone's ringing. It's that Prussian. Go and see what he wants.
POCHE. Yes, chief. (*He puts the basket* R *of the stairs and opens the door down* L)
SCHWARZ (*off*) Herein!

(POCHE *exits* L. TOURNEL *enters up* C)

TOURNEL. Good evening. Which is Monsieur Chandebise's room?
FERAILLON (*indicating the bedroom*) This way, sir. Pardon me for mentioning it, but you're not Monsieur Chandebise.
TOURNEL. I'm here to—represent his interests . . .
FERAILLON. Oh, yes—the telegram said we were to let in whoever asked for the room in his name. Madame's already there.
TOURNEL. Ah—and how does she look?
FERAILLON. Do you really need my opinion?
TOURNEL. As a matter of fact—I don't actually know her.
FERAILLON. Ah?
TOURNEL. So, before I get involved—what's she look like? Long in the tooth?
FERAILLON. Oh, no. Cheer up, sir. She may not have the sweetest character in the world, but she's certainly pretty.
TOURNEL. I didn't come here for her character . . .
FERAILLON. Of course you didn't. (*Knocking and entering the bed-room*) Well, now, here's the room . . .

(TOURNEL *enters the bedroom*)

SCHWARZ (*off*) Schnell!

(POCHE *enters* L *and moves up* RC)

POCHE. Coming right away, sir. He asked for a "shut ya hole". God knows what this is. I'll give him a vermouth!

(POCHE *picks up the log basket and exits up* C)

FERAILLON (*moving* R) No-one here! I'll find her for you. (*He knocks on the door* R)

RAYMONDE (*off*) Who's that?

FERAILLON. Your gentleman's arrived.

RAYMONDE (*off*) Good!

FERAILLON (*crossing Tournel to the bedroom door*) Madame's in there.

TOURNEL. Excellent.

FERAILLON (*going upstairs*) Good luck, sir!

(FERAILLON *exits upstairs*)

TOURNEL. Thanks. Well. This is all very pleasant. Nicely done up. Oh, the bells. If you're bored there's always target practice. Now. I know what's expected of me, but I don't know how to make it *new*. What about . . . ? Yes. I'll play a boyish prank. (*He lies on the bed and covers himself up*)

(RAYMONDE *enters* R)

RAYMONDE. So! There you . . . Well, where is he?

TOURNEL. Cuckoo!

RAYMONDE. Cuckoo. (*Moving to the bed*) You wait!

TOURNEL. Cuckoo!

RAYMONDE (*pulling the coverlet off*) Take that! (*She slaps Tournel and moves down* R)

TOURNEL. Oh!

RAYMONDE. It's not him!

TOURNEL. Raymonde, it's you!

RAYMONDE. Monsieur Tournel!

TOURNEL (*rising and moving towards Raymonde*) If I'd only known. Such a wonderful surprise.

RAYMONDE. What on earth are you doing here?

TOURNEL. What's it matter what I'm doing here? (*Moving* C) It's a great love story. A girl—is besotted with me. She saw me at a theatre and of course—the lightning struck! She wrote to me, and, out of the goodness of my heart . . .

RAYMONDE. How wrong you are!

TOURNEL. What's the matter, anyway? (*Moving* R *to Raymonde*) I don't know her! I don't even love her. But as for you—oh, my dream! My dream come true! There you are! In the flesh! All mine. The Gods are on my side. (*He puts his arm round her waist*)

RAYMONDE (*crossing below him to* C) Take your hands off me!

TOURNEL. No! No!

RAYMONDE. The letter wasn't for you! It was for my husband!

TOURNEL. Oh, come now. That's hardly very likely. I mean, he really is rather unattractive, not to say hideous. It's just that we were sitting together and this girl got us—muddled up and . . .

RAYMONDE. You're wrong again! *I* wrote the letter to my husband!

TOURNEL. *You* did?

RAYMONDE. Absolutely!

TOURNEL. You write love letters—to your husband?

RAYMONDE. I wanted to know if he'd been unfaithful—if he'd turn up here.

TOURNEL. You see! You wouldn't have me because he was unfaithful! He sent me so he's obviously faithful.

RAYMONDE. I suppose that's true.

TOURNEL. You know what he said, when he got the letter, *your* letter—he said, "What does this woman want with me? Doesn't she know I'd never be unfaithful to my wife?"

RAYMONDE. He said *that?*

TOURNEL. Yes!

RAYMONDE. Oh, I'm so happy! (*She kisses Tournel*) So happy!

TOURNEL (*returning the kiss*) Oh, Raymonde, my darling. Now—aren't you sorry you ever doubted him? You were wrong to suspect him. And you've no right not to deceive him! Poor dear fellow!

RAYMONDE. Of course—you're right! It was horrible of me to suspect him. My dear Chandebise. It was too bad of me. Please, try and forgive me.

TOURNEL (*encircling her waist*) Don't apologize. Just be mine!

RAYMONDE (*flopping in his arms*) That'll be my punishment!

TOURNEL (*kissing her all over*) Oh, Raymonde. I love you! I love you! Raymonde, my Raymonde!

RAYMONDE (*breaking free and moving down* R) Please, Tournel! Let me think for a moment!

TOURNEL (*following and grabbing her*) Don't think at all! Strike while the iron's hot!

RAYMONDE. Monsieur Tournel! Half a minute . . .

TOURNEL. Seize the moment—now, when our senses are inflamed—almost unbearably. We're off! (*Pulling her to the bed*) Come on! Come on . . .

RAYMONDE. What? Where are you taking me?

TOURNEL. There—where happiness is waiting for us.

RAYMONDE. What? There! Are you mad? (*Breaking away*) What do you take me for?

(TOURNEL *falls on the bed.* RAYMONDE *moves down* C)

TOURNEL. But I clearly understood that you agreed . . .

RAYMONDE (*moving down* R) To be your mistress, yes! But not to go to bed with you! Do you think I'm a prostitute?

TOURNEL. Well, what are we going to do?

RAYMONDE. We will have—a flirtation. Exchange looks, hold hands. I'll give you the best part of myself!

TOURNEL. Which part?

RAYMONDE. My head—and my heart.

TOURNEL. Oh! Pfhtt!

RAYMONDE. What else had you in mind?

TOURNEL (*rising and moving* L *of her*) The thoughts of every true lover. What? When all the forces of nature are drawing us together. When even your husband throws me at you! After all it was your husband who sent me . . .

RAYMONDE. My husband!

TOURNEL. Yes. Your husband. You're the only one who's complaining. Look here, Madame Chandebise, you're in a minority.

RAYMONDE (*moving below him to* C) Monsieur Tournel. Please. calm down!

TOURNEL. Do you think that'll satisfy *me?* Flirting? Exchanging looks? Half of you! And the wrong half . . .

RAYMONDE. Monsieur Tournel . . . !

TOURNEL. What can I do with your head and your heart?

RAYMONDE (*facing front*) Oh!

TOURNEL (*pacing up and down* R) No! It's a fine look-out for me! Withering in a vacuum! Continually frustrated! My reward? Little walks with madame. Taking the dog out when he feels the urge— to be taken out! (*Moving* C) Never! No! No! No!

RAYMONDE. Monsieur Tournel . . . !

TOURNEL. No! No! No! Since you don't seem to know the first rules of this game I'll have to instruct you!

RAYMONDE. My dear friend . . .

TOURNEL. Do you think I'll be made a fool of, in front of myself! Do you think I'll creep out of here the same poor idiot I came in . . .

RAYMONDE. Monsieur Tournel . . . please . . .

TOURNEL (*grabbing her*) Never! You belong to me. (*He pulls her below him and up to the bed*) And I want you!

RAYMONDE. Now then, Monsieur Tournel!

TOURNEL. No! No!

RAYMONDE (*pushing Tournel* L *and kneeling on the bed*) One step and I ring . . . (*She pushes the button*)

(*The bed revolves, bringing on* BAPTISTIN)

TOURNEL. Oh, ring! Please do! Wear out your finger! No-one'll come in here.

RAYMONDE (*as she disappears*) Help!

TOURNEL (*facing front, taking off his coat*) You can shout for help all you want! (*Leaping on top of Baptistin*) You're mine! I want you! I'll take you! Oh, Raymonde . . . My pretty one . . . ! Ah! (*He leaps up and grabs his coat*)

BAPTISTIN. Oh, my rheumatics!

TOURNEL Whatever's that?

BAPTISTIN. My poor rheumatics . . .

TOURNEL. Who let you in?

BAPTISTIN. What?

TOURNEL (*looking out of the bedroom door* C) And Raymonde. Where's she? Raymonde! (*Returning* RC) Raymonde! Raymonde!

Raymonde! Where are you? She's gone! Vanished into thin air.
Come back! Come back to me, my darling! Raymonde! (*Moving* R)
Don't disappear!

(TOURNEL *exits* R. RAYMONDE *enters from the upstage bedroom*)

RAYMONDE. Oh, my God! What's happened? Where am I?
(*Moving* L) Monsieur Tournel! Monsieur Tournel! No! I've had
enough of this hotel. I'm getting out!

(RAYMONDE *exits up* C. SCHWARZ *enters* L)

SCHWARZ. Hallo! Kellner! Hier ist niemand! Kellner! Kellner!

(RAYMONDE *enters up* C *and runs down stage*)

RAYMONDE. My husband! My husband on the staircase!

(RAYMONDE *runs off down* L)

SCHWARZ. Ach, mein Schatz, Herrlich!

(SCHWARZ *follows Raymond.* POCHE *enters up* C)

POCHE. I can't find the vermouth. I gave it to Baptistin yesterday.
(*Going to the upstage bedroom*) Baptistin. You there?
BAPTISTIN. Here I am!
POCHE (*entering the downstage bedroom*) Tell me, old man, what have
you done with the vermouth?
BAPTISTIN. In the next room. You know. On the cupboard.
POCHE. Oh, good.

(POCHE *exits into the upstage bedroom.* TOURNEL *enters* R)

TOURNEL. No-one there! Where is she? Vanished into thin air!
(*He moves* C, *as if to exit by the corridor up* C)
RAYMONDE (*off*) Stop it at once! I don't even know you!

(RAYMONDE *enters* L, *followed by* SCHWARZ)

TOURNEL. Ah! (*He comes down stage between them*)
RAYMONDE. Please stop doing that! Let me alone!
SCHWARZ. Mein Liebling, geh' nicht!
RAYMONDE. Sex maniac! (*She turns, slaps Tournel, then goes into the
bedroom*)
TOURNEL. Not again!
SCHWARZ. Danke schön!

(SCHWARZ *clicks heels and exits* L)

TOURNEL. Bitte, schön. Raymonde! Raymonde! (*He goes into the
bedroom*)
RAYMONDE (*sitting down* R) It's all too much. My husband . . .
TOURNEL. Yes.
RAYMONDE. My husband's here!
TOURNEL (*moving to Raymonde*) Oh, yes. What? Chandebise?

RAYMONDE (*rising*) Victor Emanuel. Disguised as a servant. (*Moving* c) What for? God knows! To spy on us I'm sure of that . . .

TOURNEL. It's not true!

BAPTISTIN. My rheumatics! My poor . . .

RAYMONDE. Ah!

TOURNEL. What?

RAYMONDE. In God's name! What's that?

TOURNEL. What? Oh, him. God knows. Some sort of invalid. He suddenly appeared! What the hell are you doing here?

BAPTISTIN. But you brought me in.

TOURNEL. Did I?

RAYMONDE. Get rid of him! Get rid of him at once . . .

TOURNEL. I quite agree. Go on! Get out of here!

BAPTISTIN. If I'm in the way press that button. Then I'll go back where I came from.

TOURNEL (*pressing the button*) Certainly. Right away.

(*The bed revolves, bringing on* POCHE, *with a bottle*)

RAYMONDE. That's the limit! Bringing on spectators!

TOURNEL (*moving down to Raymonde*) I promise you. I had nothing to do with it.

POCHE. Oi! Oi! What's happening now?

RAYMONDE (*moving down* R, *facing front*) Oh, my God!

TOURNEL (*facing front*) Chandebise!

RAYMONDE. My husband. I'm lost . . .

TOURNEL (*moving* L *of the bed*) My dear old friend! You mustn't believe all you see!

RAYMONDE (*moving* R *of the bed*) Don't pass judgement before you've heard us out!

POCHE. What's that?

TOURNEL. Appearances are perhaps against us. But we're completely innocent!

RAYMONDE. He's telling the truth! We never expected to meet one another . . .

TOURNEL. It was all the fault of the letter . . .

RAYMONDE. I started it all. I wrote it because . . .

TOURNEL (*kneeling*) You see? It's perfectly true.

RAYMONDE (*kneeling and putting her hand on Poche's knee*) Forgive me! I thought you were deceiving me!

POCHE. Me?

RAYMONDE. Tell me you believe me! That you don't doubt my word!

POCHE. Of course. Of course. (*Laughing*) Have they gone mad?

RAYMONDE (*backing down* R, *her hand to her heart*) I beg you, Victor Emmanuel! Don't laugh in that horrible cruel way. You hurt me so . . .

POCHE. You don't like my laugh?

RAYMONDE. I can see—you don't believe me.

TOURNEL. The circumstantial evidence may be slightly against us . . .

RAYMONDE. My God? How can we convince you?

POCHE (*rising and moving towards the door* C) Listen. I'm sorry but I've got to take the vermouth to Number Four.

RAYMONDE (*takes his arm and draws him down* C) Victor Emmanuel! What's wrong with you?

POCHE. Me?

TOURNEL. I beg of you, my old friend. At a time like this, don't let's speak of vermouth!

POCHE. But Number Four's waiting for it! Look, here's the bottle!

RAYMONDE. Enough of this play-acting. (*She kneels* C) Please. Hurt me! Punish me! Beat me! Anything better than this icy calm.

TOURNEL (*rising and kneeling a few paces* R *of Raymonde*) Yes! Beat me, too!

POCHE (*moving below Raymonde to between her and Tournel*) If you insist. But I assure you, madame . . .

RAYMONDE. Madame! Madame! No longer your little Raymonde . . .

POCHE. What?

RAYMONDE. Call me Raymonde . . .

TOURNEL. Please . . .

POCHE. What? All right. (*He kneels between them*) I'd like to. But I assure you, madame . . .

TOURNEL. Not madame. Not like a—business letter.

POCHE. Right! I assure you, Raymonde . . .

RAYMONDE. Oh, God! Tell me you believe me!

POCHE. Oh, yes. I believe you.

TOURNEL. At last.

RAYMONDE. Kiss me then, darling. Aren't you going to kiss me?

POCHE. What, me?

RAYMONDE. Kiss me! Then I'll believe you still want me.

POCHE (*moving on his knees to Raymonde*) Oh, I want you all right. (*He kisses her*)

RAYMONDE. Ah . . .

TOURNEL That's the way!

RAYMONDE. Thank you! Thank you! (*She kisses Poche's hand*)

POCHE. Lovely silky skin!

TOURNEL (*rising and facing Poche*) Me, too! Kiss me, too!

POCHE (*rising*) You, too?

TOURNEL. Then I'll know you believe me!

POCHE. All right. (*Facing front*) My God, he's a bit keen! (*He kisses Tournel*)

TOURNEL. Now I feel better.

POCHE. Me, too. But I liked it best with the lady.

RAYMONDE. "The lady."

POCHE (*moving above Raymonde to the bedroom door* C) Now I'm really going to take the vermouth to Number Four.

RAYMONDE (*rising*) Oh, not again!

TOURNEL. Look, what's this private joke?

RAYMONDE (*stopping Poche* L *of the bed*) Are you my husband or not?

POCHE. Me? Of course not. I'm the hall porter.

(RAYMONDE *and* TOURNEL *back to* R *of the bed*)

TOURNEL. What?

RAYMONDE. Victor Emmanuel—with a brain-storm!

POCHE. Not at all. Dear lady, it's all perfectly simple. You see, my name's Poche! (*He presses the button*) If you don't believe me you can ask Baptistin!

(*The bed revolves bringing on* BAPTISTIN)

RAYMONDE (*moving down* C) Baptistin?

TOURNEL (*moving down* R) Who's this . . . Baptistin?

POCHE. The poor, sick gentleman.

BAPTISTIN. Oh, my rheumatics. My poor . . .

POCHE (*sitting on the bed*) No need to go into all that! Just say who I am . . .

BAPTISTIN. Why? Don't you know?

POCHE. It is for the lady's benefit.

RAYMONDE. Yes. Who is this gentleman?

BAPTISTIN. He's Poche, of course.

TOURNEL ⎱
RAYMONDE ⎰ (*together*) Poche!

BAPTISTIN. The hall porter.

POCHE. What did I tell you?

(FERAILLON *enters downstairs*)

RAYMONDE. For heaven's sake. Could it be true?

FERAILLON. Poche! Poche!

(RAYMONDE *moves to the bedroom door*)

TOURNEL. They can't be twins. It's not possible. It's a trick . . .

FERAILLON. Poche! Where are you, Poche?

POCHE (*rising and trying to pass Raymonde*) Here, chief! I'm sorry. Call to arms! My superior officer!

RAYMONDE (*moving from the bedroom to* R *of Feraillon*) Your superior! Now we'll see. . . .

TOURNEL (*pushing Poche up stage and following Raymonde*) Get out of my way!

(POCHE *sits on the bed steps*)

RAYMONDE. Please . . .

(POCHE *rises and moves to the bedroom door* C)

FERAILLON. Yes?

RAYMONDE (*pointing at Poche*) Tell us! Who is this gentleman?

TOURNEL (*pointing at Poche*) Yes.

FERAILLON. That's Poche!

POCHE. You see!

RAYMONDE ⎱
TOURNEL ⎰ (*together*) Poche! (*They both drop their arms*)

FERAILLON (*crossing to Poche and kicking him round in a full circle*)
Poche! Here, with a bottle in his hand! You dog's dinner! You
animal! You soak!

POCHE. See what I told you?

FERAILLON. You starting up again?

RAYMONDE } (*together*) What?
TOURNEL

POCHE. But it's for Number Four.

FERAILLON (*taking the bottle from Poche and kicking him round again*)
I'll give you Number Four.

POCHE. Yes, chief.

FERAILLON. Take that!

POCHE. You see——

FERAILLON. And that!

POCHE. —just as I told you——

FERAILLON. And that!

POCHE. —I could only be Poche!

FERAILLON. And get the hell out of here at the double!

(POCHE *exits up* C)

So sorry about that. My porter's a sort of alcholic mess.

(FERAILLON *exits up* L)

RAYMONDE. The porter?

TOURNEL. Raymonde!

RAYMONDE. What?

TOURNEL. We have kissed the hall porter.

RAYMONDE. Just what I was thinking.

TOURNEL. I'm shattered! As like as two peas. Is it possible?

RAYMONDE. But—look at what happened! Those kicks! Victor
Emmanuel might want to fool me, but he'd surely never stand being
kicked up the . . .

TOURNEL Back.

RAYMONDE. Yes.

TOURNEL. Obviously.

RAYMONDE (*moving to the stool down* C) All this emotion! I'm dry as
a bone. (*Sitting*) For pity's sake—water!

TOURNEL (*searching his pockets*) Where did I put it?

RAYMONDE. In the bedroom! (*She rises*)

TOURNEL (*moving into the bedroom*) Water! Yes, for God's sake,
water. Where's water?

BAPTISTIN. In the bathroom.

TOURNEL. Thanks.

(TOURNEL *exits* R. RAYMONDE *enters the bedroom*)

RAYMONDE. Can you imagine? My husband a hall porter! (*She
sits down* R)

(POCHE *enters* C *with a full log basket and moves to the stairs.* EUGÉNIE
enters downstairs. POCHE *drops a log on the stairs*)

BAPTISTIN. That's just like life—isn't it?
POCHE. Eugénie, put that back for me.
EUGÉNIE (*doing so*) There you are, love.
RAYMONDE. I must have water.

(RAYMONDE *exits* R. CAMILLE *and* ANTOINETTE *enter up* C, CAMILLE *leading her by the hand. He is now wearing the palate and his speech is normal. As he speaks he moves down* C, ANTOINETTE *moves down* L)

CAMILLE. This way, my little chick. This is the scene of the crime, and your great big Camille's going to love every delicious minute of it. They must have kept us a room!
POCHE (*moving between Camille and Antoinette*) Can I help you, sir?
CAMILLE. Yes, I want to know—Victor Emmanuel!

(CAMILLE *runs into the upstage bedroom* C)

ANTOINETTE. Sir!

(ANTOINETTE *runs off down* L)

POCHE (*going upstairs*) What's wrong with everyone today? They keep calling me Victor Emmanuel.

(POCHE *exits upstairs.* EUGÉNIE *exits up* L. TOURNEL *and* RAYMONDE *enter* R)

TOURNEL. Feeling better now?
RAYMONDE (*moving to the table below the door* C) Yes! No! I don't know. All this emotion! I think I'm going to faint.
TOURNEL (*moving to Raymonde*) Please! Don't!
RAYMONDE. I'm not doing it for pleasure!
TOURNEL. Of course not. (*Taking Raymonde to the bed*) You ought to lie down a moment. Come on, stretch out on the bed.
RAYMONDE. I won't say no. (*She lies on Baptistin*)
RAYMONDE ⎱ (*together*) Ah!
BAPTISTIN ⎰

(RAYMONDE *jumps up and runs down* C. TOURNEL *runs down* R)

TOURNEL. Whatever is it? What? You again! You're always here!
BAPTISTIN. But you brought me in!
RAYMONDE. It's too much. Don't argue about it. Get rid of him! (*She moves on to the bed steps*)
TOURNEL (*pressing the button*) All right. Now! Back to where you belong!

(*The bed revolves bringing on* CAMILLE *under the coverlet*)

RAYMONDE. It's very rude to keep whirling into people's bedrooms. (*She falls on to Camille, then leaps up*) Ah . . . !
TOURNEL (*catching her*) Look out! Here!
CAMILLE. What's happening? Help! It's an earthquake! Oh, dear . . .
TOURNEL ⎱ (*together*) Camille!
RAYMONDE ⎰

(TOURNEL *and* RAYMONDE *run from the bedroom to* LC)

CAMILLE. I'm terribly sorry. My bed ran away with me.
RAYMONDE. It can't be him. It speaks . . .
TOURNEL. It speaks. It's not him! It's not!
CAMILLE (*rising*) The bed ran away with me!
RAYMONDE. Let's go.

(RAYMONDE *exits up* C)

TOURNEL. Yes. Let's go!

(TOURNEL *exits up* C)

CAMILLE (*looking through the door* C) Tournel and Raymonde!
What're they up to? Suppose they recognized me! What's happened
to Antoinette?

(*There is a commotion off down* L)

(*Moving* L) What's she doing in there? Antoinette! (*He opens the door*)
Good God!

(CAMILLE *exits down* L. RAYMONDE *enters up* C, *followed by* TOUR-
NEL)

RAYMONDE. Etienne! Etienne's here!
TOURNEL. The butler! My God, what a circus!

(RAYMONDE *and* TOURNEL *run off* L. CAMILLE *and* SCHWARZ
enter L. SCHWARZ *backs* CAMILLE *to up* LC, *below the stairs*)

SCHWARZ. Geh' weg! Geh' weg!
CAMILLE. But excuse me, sir . . .
SCHWARZ. Ach, verpflucht! (*He slaps Camille's face*)

(CAMILLE's *palate falls on the floor*)

Geh' doch weg, sage ich!
CAMILLE (*bending to pick it up*) My palate! My palate!
SCHWARZ (*grabbing Camille by the collar and pants*) Na, also! (*Kicking
Camille towards the upstage bedroom*) So ein Unverschämtheit!

(CAMILLE, *kicked by* SCHWARZ, *exits to the upstage bedroom*)

(*Moving* L) Ach! Ich bin's, mein Liebling!

(SCHWARZ *exits down* L. ETIENNE *enters up* C)

ETIENNE. No-one about? (*He picks up the palate*) Quite a nice bit
of work. It's damp . . .

(EUGÉNIE *enters up* L *and moves to Etienne*)

EUGÉNIE. Did you want something, sir?
ETIENNE. Yes, miss, in the first place I've just found this valuable
little object on the floor. For the moment I find its exact nature
something of a mystery . . .

(CAMILLE *enters*)

CAMILLE. Oh, dear, what has happened to my silver roof?
EUGÉNIE. What a funny looking thing! Sort of ancient Egyptian brooch.
CAMILLE (*facing front*) My God! Etienne!

(CAMILLE *exits to the upstage bedroom*)

EUGÉNIE. A lady must have dropped it. I'll hand it in downstairs.
ETIENNE. Very right and proper. And now tell me, has there been a lady asking for Monsieur Chandebise's room?
EUGÉNIE. Yes . . .
ETIENNE. And where is—this certain lady?
EUGÉNIE. Oh, I'm not allowed to tell . . .
ETIENNE. I've got to see her! Her husband might intrude on her at any moment. He's a fiend and he'll certainly do her in.
EUGÉNIE. Good God!
ETIENNE. I've got to warn her!
EUGÉNIE. If it's like that—I saw her go in there. (*She points down* L)
ETIENNE (*putting on his hat and moving down* L) Good enough! (*He knocks*)
SCHWARZ (*off*) Geh' doch weg!
ETIENNE (*opening the door*) Begging your pardon—my wife!

(ETIENNE *exits down* L. *A commotion is heard in the room*)

EUGÉNIE. What's going on?

(ANTOINETTE *enters* L *and runs up* C)

ANTOINETTE. Etienne. Etienne's here! Help me! Help!

(ANTOINETTE *exits up* C. ETIENNE *enters*)

ETIENNE (*running up* C) Stop that woman!

(SCHWARZ, *in his pants, enters* L)

SCHWARZ (*grabbing Etienne and swinging him round*) Ach, du dummer Trottel!
ETIENNE. Ow!
SCHWARZ (*shaking Etienne*) Ich werde dich umbringen.
ETIENNE. She's my wife! You've got no business to . . .
SCHWARZ. Na!
ETIENNE. Please. Leave me alone!
SCHWARZ (*throwing Etienne on the floor*) Also und jetzt, geh' weg!

(SCHWARZ *exits down* L)

ETIENNE. It's not right. I'm the wronged husband. I'm not the one who ought to be hit. (*He gets up*)
EUGÉNIE. If you'd told me you were the husband . . .

(POCHE *comes downstairs with the log basket*)

ETIENNE. You think I knew? It's too bloody much. Me! A gentleman's gentleman! And deceived! You little slut! Just you wait, that's all! Just you wait! (*He turns and sees Poche*)

POCHE. What is it?

ETIENNE. Sir—you're—carrying a log basket!

POCHE. Yes. I am carrying a log basket. Why not?

ETIENNE. Oh, sir! My dear sir. I've been deceived. My wife's unfaithful, sir!

POCHE. Bad luck!

ETIENNE. She did it in there, sir. With a Prussian . . .

POCHE. Herr Shutyourhole.

ETIENNE. He didn't tell me his name. But, as you're here, sir. As you don't need my services, may I give chase, sir? May I catch the little devil, and then—and then—I have your permission, sir?

POCHE. Go ahead.

ETIENNE. Thank you, sir. I'm so grateful. (*Going up* C) Look out, you slut—I'm coming . . .

(ETIENNE *exits up* C)

POCHE. I don't know if it's something they've eaten, but it's my opinion they're all barmy.

(*The buzzer sounds, Room 7*)

LUCIENNE (*off* C) Mind where you're going.

EUGÉNIE. Someone's ringing! (*Moving to the board*) It's for you! (*She moves down* C)

POCHE. For me—good, somebody wants me! Coming! Coming!

(POCHE *exits up* L. LUCIENNE *enters up* C)

LUCIENNE. Extraordinary. I could have sworn that was Chandebise's butler.

EUGÉNIE. Can I help you, madame?

LUCIENNE (*moving down* L *of Lucienne*) Oh, yes. Yes. A man nearly knocked me flying on the stairs. Wasn't he Monsieur Chandebise's butler?

EUGÉNIE. That's possible! He asked for a room booked in that name, madame. He said he came to warn a woman to make herself scarce as her husband was after her. And when he met the lady it turned out he was her husband, and he was after her, madame, and —it's a bit of a muddle, quite frankly!

LUCIENNE. I don't understand a word of it.

EUGÉNIE. I'm only tell you what I saw.

LUCIENNE. Anyway—which is the room booked in Monsieur Chandebise's name?

EUGÉNIE. The room boo . . . Oh, it's that one. (*She points* R *to the downstage bedroom*)

LUCIENNE (*crossing Eugénie to the bedroom door*) Good. I'm going in there . . .

EUGÉNIE. That's quite all right. (*Moving to the stairs*) I've been told to let anyone in who asks for it.

(EUGÉNIE *exits upstairs*)

LUCIENNE. Thanks. (*She knocks on the bedroom door*)

(CAMILLE *enters from the upstage bedroom and moves* L)

CAMILLE. I do wish I could find my silver roof.
LUCIENNE. Nobody there! (*She knocks again*)
CAMILLE. Madame Hisangua! Oh God! Whatever next?

(CAMILLE *exits up* C)

LUCIENNE (*entering the bedroom*) No-one here? It's not possible. Raymonde said: "I'll expose my husband between five o'clock and ten past. Come at half past and it'll all be over." Didn't she wait for me? Let's look in here . . .

(LUCIENNE *exits* R. CAMILLE *enters up* C)

CAMILLE. Victor Emmanuel! It's Victor Emmanuel!

(CAMILLE *exits to the upstage bedroom.* LUCIENNE *enters* R)

LUCIENNE. It's very odd! Never mind, I'm going . . .

(CHANDEBISE *enters up* C)

CHANDEBISE. Who should I ask for? Ah . . . You!
LUCIENNE. Monsieur Chandebise!
CHANDEBISE. At last, I've found you . . .
LUCIENNE. What's the matter with you?
CHANDEBISE. Did you see Etienne by any chance?
LUCIENNE. Why?
CHANDEBISE. Because I sent him to tell you—you see I had a dinner. But then I discovered—my dinner's not till tomorrow! So I—I—rushed here to tell you . . .
LUCIENNE. Tell me what?
CHANDEBISE. Oh, my poor child. What utter madness—to fall in love with me. *Me?*
LUCIENNE. *What?*
CHANDEBISE. I do understand. (*Taking her hand*) Of course I understand. Were you afraid to sign your adorable letter?
LUCIENNE. What letter?
CHANDEBISE. The one you wrote to arrange our little—rendez-vous?
LUCIENNE. Oh! But what makes you think that was me?
CHANDEBISE. I didn't know who it was at first. But I showed it to your husband and . . .
LUCIENNE (*removing her hand*) You did *what?*
CHANDEBISE. He knew your handwriting at once . . .
LUCIENNE. What are you trying to tell me?
CHANDEBISE. Of course, now he's perfectly capable of killing you!
LUCIENNE (*moving below him to down* L) Madre de Dios! Where is he?
CHANDEBISE. Probably just about to—breathe down our necks!

LUCIENNE. Our necks! Oh, my God! Don't just stand there! (*Running up* C) Run away! Help . . . !

(LUCIENNE *exits up* C)

CHANDEBISE. Oh, the madness of love!

(CHANDEBISE *exits up* C. OLYMPE *enters up* L)

OLYMPE. Eugénie! Eugénie! Where's that girl got to?

(CHANDEBISE *enters up* C)

CHANDEBISE. It's him! Histangua. Abandon ship!

(LUCIENNE *enters up* C)

LUCIENNE. My husband! I'm lost!
OLYMPE. What's happening?
CHANDEBISE (*pulling Olympe round to* C) Out of my way!

(CHANDEBISE *exits down* L)

OLYMPE. What?
LUCIENNE (*pushing Olympe below the stairs*) Out of my way!

(LUCIENNE *runs to the bedroom and exits* R)

OLYMPE. But, madame . . .

(RAYMONDE *enters up* L)

RAYMONDE. Oh, let's go! I won't breathe again till we're out of here. Out of my way! (*She pulls Olympe round in a circle* L)
OLYMPE. Ah . . .

(TOURNEL *enters up* L)

TOURNEL. Yes. Quick. This way. But for God's sake—out of our way! (*He pushes Olympe down* L)

(RAYMONDE *and* TOURNEL *exit up* C)

OLYMPE. Are we on fire? What's going . . . ?
HOMENIDES (*off* C) Let me find them! Let me find them! Then I can kill them! Then I can strangle them with my bare hands!
OLYMPE (*moving to the stairs*) Now what is it?

(RAYMONDE *enters up* C *and runs up* L)

RAYMONDE. Homenides de Histangua! Out of my way!

(RAYMONDE *pushes Olympe up* C *and exits up* L)

OLYMPE. Ah . . .

(TOURNEL *enters up* C *and pushes Olympe down* C)

TOURNEL. Damned dago! You're always in the way!

(TOURNEL *exits up* L. OLYMPE *staggers down* L)

OLYMPE. Oh, dear—oh, dear—what's—what's this?

(HOMENIDES *enters up* C *and moves down* C)

HOMENIDES. So Tournel with a woman! It must be my wife—
the mitherable strumpet! (*He moves up* LC)
OLYMPE (*stopping Homenides* L *of the stairs*) Excuse me. Where are
you going, sir?
HOMENIDES. To kill the both of them. With my bare hands! Get
out of my way! (*He pushes Olympe down stage*)

(HOMENIDES *exits up* L)

OLYMPE (*staggering down* C) Kill them! Oh, my God! Help! Help!
Help! (*She sits down* C)

(FERAILLON *and* EUGÉNIE *enter downstairs*)

FERAILLON. What's all the noise about?
OLYMPE (*rising*) An escaped lunatic! He says he's going to kill
them!
FERAILLON. What? (*He moves up* L)
OLYMPE. Ah—Ah—Aha!
EUGÉNIE (*running to support Olympe from behind*) Help!
FERAILLON (*moving* C *and pointing up* L) All right. Take her in
there. Give her a whiff of smelling salts.

(*A commotion breaks out down* L)

EUGÉNIE. Yes, sir!

(EUGÉNIE *and* OLYMPE *exit up* L)

FERAILLON (*hurrying to Schwarz's room*) War's almost breaking out
in there.

(SCHWARZ *enters down* L, *pulls* CHANDEBISE *out of the room and
spins him across* R. CHANDEBISE *bumps into Feraillon on his way across,
and lands on the stool* C)

SCHWARZ (*as he pulls Chandebise out*) Geh' doch von meiner Tür
weg!
CHANDEBISE. No! No!
FERAILLON. What's going on here?

(SCHWARZ *exits down* L)

FERAILLON (*moving to Chandebise*) Poche! You back again?
CHANDEBISE (*rising*) What did you say?
FERAILLON. You useless nitwit! (*He kicks Chandebise round in a
circle*)
CHANDEBISE. What are you doing?
FERAILLON. Dog's dinner!
CHANDEBISE. But . . .
FERAILLON. A pig could teach you manners!
CHANDEBISE. Listen to me, my man!
FERAILLON. *What?*

CHANDEBISE (*putting on his hat and taking off his gloves*) I am Monsieur Victor Emmanuel Chandebise, managing director for all France of the Boston Life Insurance Company.

FERAILLON (*facing front*) Tight as a drum! Soaked, sozzled, saturated . . .

CHANDEBISE. Sir. (*He strikes him across the chest with his gloves*) My seconds will call on you. (*He moves up* C)

FERAILLON. Oh, yes? Well, take one of these for each of your seconds! (*He kicks Chandebise round in a circle again*)

CHANDEBISE. Oh—oh . . .

FERAILLON. And that for Monsieur Chandebise!

CHANDEBISE. Oh!

FERAILLON. And that! And that! (*He finishes* L *of Chandebise*)

CHANDEBISE. That'll be quite enough from you! (*He pulls his arm away*)

FERAILLON (*pulling Chandebise's jacket off his shoulder*) What's the idea?

CHANDEBISE. If you don't mind!

FERAILLON (*turning Chandebise round and taking his jacket off*) This your idea of a joke? Parading in civies?

CHANDEBISE. You're going too far . . .

FERAILLON (*taking off Chandebise's hat*) You can do without that as well. (*He moves to the coat-rack down* L, *hangs up the hat and jacket, and takes down the uniform cap and coat*)

CHANDEBISE (*facing front*) My God! It's a raving maniac!

FERAILLON. Get your cap on now! (*He puts the cap on Chandebise's head*)

CHANDEBISE. No! No!

FERAILLON. And your jacket! (*He gets one of Chandebise's arms in the sleeve*)

CHANDEBISE. I won't wear it! (*He moves down* L)

FERAILLON. Won't wear your uniform? I'll tell you when to wear your uniform. Get dressed—at the double.

CHANDEBISE. Yes! Yes, sir! (*He puts on the coat*) Yes . . .

FERAILLON. Now! Dis-miss. To your room! Like greased bloody lightning! (*He moves up* L)

CHANDEBISE. Yes, sir. Yes. It's a raving—raving . . .

FERAILLON. What did you say? You want another touch of my boot?

CHANDEBISE (*moving to the stairs*) No! No!

FERAILLON. All right then!

CHANDEBISE (*facing front*) Maniac! Complete maniac!

FERAILLON. Will you—shog off!

(CHANDEBISE *exits upstairs*)

You see! The terrible effect of vermouth! Still dead drunk! It's sad, when you find a decent servant, he has to turn out a hopeless sot . . .

(EUGÉNIE *enters up* L)

EUGÉNIE. Oh, there you are, sir.

FERAILLON. What is it now?

EUGÉNIE. Madame's got the screaming tiff-taffs . . .

FERAILLON. Oh, my God, what's next on the menu I wonder? What do you want me to do about it? What do you take me for? An army nurse?

EUGÉNIE. For Heaven's sake, sir, what are we going to do about madame?

FERAILLON. In case of shock I always recommend a quick slap around the chops. She'll find that very reassuring. Try that.

EUGÉNIE. Thank you very much. I'd get a quick slap back.

FERAILLON. Yes, might do you a bit of good. (*Moving up* L) All right. Run up to Number Ten and ask Doctor Finache to come and look at her. At a convenient moment!

EUGÉNIE. At the double, sir.

FERAILLON. What a bloody nuisance. (*Going out up* L) Now then, my precious. Feeling a little bit seedy, are we?

(FERAILLON *exits up* L. *As soon as he is out of sight,* POCHE *enters up* L, *singing the* "*Marseillaise*", *and moves to the coat-rack* L)

POCHE. Now—off to the post office. Well! What joker's pinched my uniform? Cheeky bastard! (*He takes Chandebise's hat and coat*) He's left his hat and coat instead of mine. (*Putting them on*) Not a bad fit, for going to the post office. (*Moving up* C) I'll give them back when he hands over mine.

(*The buzzer sounds—Number 11*)

Good! Someone wants me. They do love me here! Coming! Coming!

(POCHE *exits up* L. EUGÉNIE *and* FINACHE *enter downstairs and move below them*)

EUGÉNIE (*as she comes down*) This way, Doctor.

FINACHE. You don't imagine I came here to practice medicine? What's the matter with your mistress?

EUGÉNIE. Nothing much. Just the screaming tiff-taffs.

FINACHE. Whatever's that?

EUGÉNIE. A sort of blue fit. She had a fright and . . .

FINACHE. A fright? Why not say so?

EUGÉNIE. It froze her blood! Now it's spread to her nerves, I should imagine.

FINACHE. And you interrupted me for that? Get a good big soda-water siphon and give her a squirt. That'll calm her down.

EUGÉNIE. You'd better see her. (*Moving up* L) You've gone to all this trouble . . .

FINACHE. Yes, I have!

EUGÉNIE. This way, Doctor . . .

(EUGÉNIE *and* FINACHE *exit up* L. CHANDEBISE *comes downstairs*)

CHANDEBISE (*moving* C) The maniac's gone. What I've been through! If that's how he welcomes his guests, I can't see them

coming back a second time! What a maniac! (*Moving* L) Good
heavens! Where's my jacket? And my hat! He hung them there!
They've vanished. (*He looks under the table*)

(RAYMONDE *and* TOURNEL *enter up* L)

RAYMONDE. We've given him the slip! Quick, call a cab!
TOURNEL (*seeing Chandebise*) Yes. Here's the porter.
RAYMONDE (*crossing below Tournel to Chandebise*) The hall porter . . .
CHANDEBISE. What a thing to happen . . .
RAYMONDE. Quick, Poche. A cab!
CHANDEBISE. What?
TOURNEL. A cab!
CHANDEBISE. My wife!
RAYMONDE. My husband! It is him. (*Running up* C) It is . . .

(RAYMONDE *exits up* C)

CHANDEBISE. And with Tournel!
TOURNEL. It really is! (*He backs to* C *and sits on the stool*)
CHANDEBISE (*following Tournel and pushing him down each time he rises*)
What are you doing here? You! What are you doing with *my wife?*
TOURNEL (*rising*) You know quite well!
CHANDEBISE (*pushing him down*) What? What do I know?
TOURNEL (*rising*) We just explained it all to you.
CHANDEBISE (*pushing him down*) Oh, yes! You explained it all!
What did you explain? Answer me! Will you answer . . . ?
TOURNEL (*rising*) Now, just a moment . . .

(FERAILLON *enters up* L *and moves down* C)

FERAILLON. Haven't we had enough of this bloody row! Poche!
CHANDEBISE. The maniac!
FERAILLON. Poche!

(TOURNEL *exits up* L. FERAILLON *kicks Chandebise round in a circle*)

FERAILLON. You animal!
CHANDEBISE. Eh! Oh! Help!
FERAILLON. Beast!
CHANDEBISE. Oh!
FERAILLON. Pig!
CHANDEBISE (*running to the stairs*) Now then, my man. Look here.
FERAILLON (*following him*) Haven't you had enough?
CHANDEBISE. Yes! Yes! Quite enough. Help! Help me! Help!
There's a maniac. A raving maniac . . .

(CHANDEBISE *runs up the stairs*)

FERAILLON (*following*) I'll give you maniac, you vermouth besotted sponge! Back to your cell till tomorrow morning. Go and sleep
it off. Double! Double! And twice as quick as that, you dozy bastard!

(CHANDEBISE *and* FERAILLON *exit upstairs.* SCHWARZ *enters down*
L, *putting on his jacket, and moves up* C)

Schwarz. Verpflucht nochmal! Ich muss selbst sehen, ob diese Sache ewig dauern wird!

(Schwarz *exits up* c. Camille *enters from the upstage bedroom and moves down* l. Lucienne *enters* r *and moves to the bedroom door* c)

Camille. Nobody about. Oh, I do wish I could find my silver roof!

Lucienne. It's gone quiet again!

Camille (*seeing Lucienne and moving to the corridor up* c) Madame Histangua!

Lucienne (*closing the bedroom door behind her*) My husband must have gone.

(Lucienne *and* Camille *scream on seeing each other.* Lucienne *grabs Camille by the arm and pulls him down* l)

Oh, Camille—please! Don't leave me. My husband's breathing down my neck. With a revolver! He wants to kill everyone!

Camille. Good God!

Lucienne. I beg you. Don't leave me!

Camille. No! No! I won't . . .

Homenides (*off upstairs*) Where are the wretcheth? Where are you hiding?

(Lucienne *and* Camille *scream*)

Lucienne. My husband!

Camille. That's him!

Lucienne ⎫
Camille ⎬ (*together*) Let's run!

(Lucienne *and* Camille *run up* c. Schwarz *enters up* c. Camille *rushes into the bedroom downstage and puts his back against the door.* Lucienne *runs into the bedroom down* l)

Schwarz. Ach Mensch! Was für ein hübsches Mädchen!

(Schwarz *exits down* l, *taking off his jacket,* Homenides *rushes downstairs*)

Homenides. Where are they? I want to kill them! To slay them both! Just tell me! Where is the room of Chandebise? Is everybody dead?

(Homenides *runs out up* c. Poche *enters up* l *and moves* r *of the stairs*)

Poche. Who's making all this noise?

(Lucienne *enters down* l, *backing.* Schwarz *follows her*)

Schwarz. Sei' lieb, mein Schatz. Komm zuruck.

Lucienne. Kindly stop that suggestive behaviour! (*She slaps Schwarz's face*)

Schwarz. Nochmal! Ach, wie ist das scheusslich!

(SCHWARZ *spins round and exits* L. POCHE *comes down stage* R *of* Lucienne)

POCHE. Good shot!
LUCIENNE (*falling into his arms*) Monsieur Chandebise!
POCHE. What?
LUCIENNE. God's sent you—to save my life!
POCHE. What's the matter, madame?
LUCIENNE. My husband's after me. He wants to kill me!
POCHE. What's that again?
LUCIENNE. Save me! Save me!
POCHE (*pulling her up* C) Come on, then. This way out.

(LUCIENNE *and* POCHE *exit up* C)

HOMENIDES (*off up* C) Ah! Caramba! Caught you!

(LUCIENNE *enters up* C, *runs down* C *and tries to open the bedroom door, which* CAMILLE *is barring*)

LUCIENNE. It's him! Open, please!
CAMILLE. No-one's coming in here!

(POCHE *enters up* C. LUCIENNE *runs down* L)

POCHE. Hurry up! Not in there, Herr Shutyourhole.
LUCIENNE (*running* C) Where then?
POCHE (*moving to the upstage bedroom*) In there! Baptistin's room!

(LUCIENNE *exits into the upstage bedroom.* POCHE *follows and shuts the door behind them.* HOMENIDES *enters* C)

HOMENIDES. Don't bother to hide yourselves. I've theen you. Death . . . (*He stops short up* C)

(EUGÉNIE *enters up* L *and moves to Homenides*)

EUGÉNIE. Did you want something, sir?
HOMENIDES. I want Chandebise! And the woman with him!
EUGÉNIE (*pointing to the downstage bedroom*) In there, sir. He's mad!

(EUGÉNIE *exits up* L)

HOMENIDES (*knocking on the bedroom door*) Open up! So I can kill you!
CAMILLE. Nobody at home.
HOMENIDES. Will you open up! (*As he counts, he shoulders the door three times*) Uno! Dos! Tres!

(*On the third count,* CAMILLE *dives to the chair down* R. HOMENIDES *rushes into the bedroom and exits* R. *There is a glass crash off* R, *then* HOMENIDES *re-enters and stands over Camille*)

My wife. Just you give me my wife! So I can kill her. Tho' I can slay her! I'm a dead shot. (*Crossing* C) See that target? (*Indicating the bed button*) Toro! (*He produces his revolver and fires at the button*) Bull's-eye!

(*The bed revolves, bringing on* POCHE *and* LUCIENNE. HOMENIDES, *returning to Camille, does not see this*)

Caramba! When I find her, she dies! Hasta la meurte!
CAMILLE. I promise. I haven't got her. Search me!
LUCIENNE. My husband!

(LUCIENNE *rushes out of the bedroom and exits up* C, *followed by* POCHE)

HOMENIDES. My wife! (*He fires at the bedroom door, then rushes from the room*)

(FERAILLON *comes running downstairs, meeting* HOMENIDES C)

FERAILLON. Do I hear shots? War's broken out! In my hotel? Now then, what's going on here exactly? Oh, my God, apprehend him! A madman! A stark raving . . . Poche! Eugénie! Apprehend him!

(FERAILLON *and* HOMENIDES *struggle* C. *More shots are fired.* SCHWARZ *enters* L *and moves* C)

Stop the carnage! Ah—got you, my beauty! You're not getting away with this. Police! Send for the police!

(*During the ensuing chaos,* OLYMPE, EUGÉNIE *and two* MEN *and two* WOMEN *guests rush on from the corridors and down the stairs to join in the turmoil. In the bedroom,* CAMILLE *jumps on the bed and under the coverlet. The bed revolves continuously, bringing on* BAPTISTIN *and* CAMILLE *in turn, both shrieking. All the following speeches are spoken simultaneously*)

	Barbaric behaviour! Ou uncouth savage, you! Police! Police! Thank God—the maid. Got my orders, have you? Jump to it . . .
EUGENIE	All right, all right—what's the matter now? Good heavens, who's he got hold of there? Look, sir— look. It's the chief—he's got himself in the soup, all right. Oh, no, it's a bit too much. I'm not staying in this monkey house a moment longer, Madame! Madame! Look, sir, Madame! Madame!
IST MAN	(*to* IST *Woman*) Don't be afraid, my little darling. Your Paul's here to look after you. What's going on down there? Will you kindly stop this ridiculous horseplay! What'ee you waiting for? Stop it! Stop it! Mannerless apes. And this is meant to be a quiet little hotel. It'll be a long time before I set foot in here again. Fernande, where are you? Please! Answer me, Fernande . . . Fernande!
OLYMPE	I thought I heard a noise! Aaaah! Help! Help! Feraillon! He's going to kill me! Help! I can feel it coming on again! I'm about to faint dead away . . . Eugénie! Help me! Eugénie!

1st Woman ⎧ Can't you see? Help! They're going to kill us. To
           ⎪ slaughter us—in our beds! I told you I didn't
           ⎪ want to come here! Don't shoot—not at me!
           ⎪ Not at me. Help! Paul, don't just stand there,
           ⎪ save me!
2nd Man   ⎨ Don't make such a noise! Please—try to be quiet.
           ⎪ What's happening, exactly? Stop it—come on,
           ⎪ this way, we're getting out—come along. Police!
           ⎪ Police!
2nd Woman ⎪ My husband! I know it's my husband! Oh, please!
           ⎪ Edouard, don't shoot! I beg you, don't shoot!
           ⎪ Aaaah—it's not him! Help, help! This is the
           ⎩ absolute limit! Help!

Eventually Homenides *is overpowered and forced out up* c, Olympe
faints down c, Eugénie *bends over her, the bed stops revolving with*
Baptistin *in view screaming, as the lights* Black-Out *and—*

the Curtain *falls*

ACT III

SCENE— *The Chandebises' drawing-room. Half an hour later.*
As the CURTAIN *rises,* ANTOINETTE *enters up* C *and moves down stage, doing up her blouse buttons.*

ANTOINETTE. Help! Etienne's back! I'll never have time—I'm all fingers and thumbs! Right! Now we'll see!
ETIENNE (*off* C) Antoinette! Antoinette!
ANTOINETTE. Oh! (*She runs to the doors up* C *and bolts them*)
ETIENNE (*off*) Antoinette!
ANTOINETTE (*grabbing her apron from the sofa and putting it on*) Help!
ETIENNE (*off*) Antoinette! Will you open! The little slut's locked herself in! Just wait!
ANTOINETTE. Quick! (*She unbolts the doors, then runs down* L)

(ANTOINETTE *exits down* L. ETIENNE *enters up* R *and moves down* C)

ETIENNE. Antoinette! Where's she got to? Antoinette!

(ANTOINETTE *enters down* L)

ANTOINETTE (*moving to the table*) Was it you making that extraordinary noise?
ETIENNE. Of course it was. What's the idea? Locking yourself in?
ANTOINETTE. What?
ETIENNE. I want to know why you were locked in.
ANTOINETTE. Me? Of course I wasn't locked in.
ETIENNE (*moving up* C *and opening the door*) Now look! That's peculiar . . .
ANTOINETTE (*picking up the magazines from the table and moving* R) The wonders of science! Etienne learns how to open a door! (*She puts the magazines on the small table* RC)
ETIENNE (*moving* L *of the sofa*) Never mind. The door's unimportant. Just you tell me—what were you doing at the Hotel Coq d'Or.
ANTOINETTE. What did you say?
ETIENNE. The Hotel Coq d'Or.
ANTOINETTE. What on earth is "The Hotel Coq d'Or?
ETIENNE. What on earth? Oh, very good! But I've got you now. It wasn't half an hour ago—that I caught you there . . .
ANTOINETTE. You caught me? *Me?*
ETIENNE. Yes, you!
ANTOINETTE (*sitting on the sofa*) I haven't moved out of here!
ETIENNE. A likely story!
ANTOINETTE. It's perfectly true.
ETIENNE. I thought you'd do better than that. I mean something like "It was my long lost twin sister" or "I just popped in to collect

the fish". But not "I wasn't there". (*Moving down* L) Not a bare-faced denial.

ANTOINETTE. I can't say what didn't happen.

ETIENNE (*moving* L *of the sofa*) You miserable sinner! I saw you with my own eyes . . .

ANTOINETTE (*rising*) What does that prove?

ETIE ᴠE. Oh!

ANTOINETTE. It doesn't matter to me if you saw me or not. I still wasn't there.

ETIENNE (*moving down* C) The nerve! The pure ice cold! So! So, I didn't catch you there? Half naked—all wrapped around by an Alsatian wolf-hound.

ANTOINETTE. Me?

ETIENNE. Yes, you! You! And he didn't get violent with me either, I don't suppose!

ANTOINETTE. Me, with an Alsatian gentleman? It's ridiculous. I don't even speak the language.

ETIENNE. Oh, yes! Very convincing. Certain things are beyond the barriers of language. Certain things—can be explained by signs! So—you weren't being hugged by a Hun?

ANTOINETTE. Never moved out of the house.

ETIENNE (*moving* L) God Almighty! Subtle little bitch! She lies like a respectable woman! So you never moved out of the house? All right. We'll find out. (*He moves up* C)

ANTOINETTE. What are we going to do?

ETIENNE. Ask the concierge.

ANTOINETTE (*moving up to Etienne*) The conceirge!

ETIENNE. He'll tell me, if you went out!

ANTOINETTE ⎫ ⎧ You're out of your mind! You can't in-
　　　　　　 ⎪ ⎪ involve Monsieur Plommard in a
　　　　　　 ⎪ ⎪ ridiculous family squabble. Do you
　　　　　　 ⎬ (*together*) ⎨ want the whole street to laugh at
　　　　　　 ⎪ ⎪ you?
ETIENNE 　　⎪ ⎪ That's got you, hasn't it? You didn't
　　　　　　 ⎪ ⎪ think of that. Now you're hooked,
　　　　　　 ⎭ ⎩ clever puss!

ANTOINETTE (*beating on Etienne's chest*) Listen, Etienne!

ETIENNE. I'm not listening . . . (*He pushes her down stage*)

ANTOINETTE (*moving below the table*) Oh, do what you like! (*She leans on the table*)

(ETIENNE *moves into the hall picks up the telephone and leans on the door jamb*)

ETIENNE. Hullo . . . Oh hullo, Monsieur Plommard. Good! . . . Slightly odd request, old man, but I need the information. Did you happen to notice what time my wife went out this afternoon? . . . What? She didn't go out? It's not possible! . . . Perhaps she slipped past you . . . What? She had a bite to eat with you. Onion soup! Oh, yes. I see. No-one's in for dinner up here so she just popped down. Oh, yes, indeed . . . Really? You don't say so . . . ?

ANTOINETTE. Five francs—that call cost me!
ETIENNE. I can't understand it! It's incredible . . . All right.
Thanks, old man. Sorry to bother you. (*He replaces the receiver and moves* c)
ANTOINETTE (*turning up stage*) And, so . . . ?
ETIENNE (*moving down* R) Let me alone! What am I? Soft in the head? Short-sighted?
ANTOINETTE (*moving up* c) What fools jealousy can make of us!
ETIENNE (*moving above the sofa*) Yes . . . all right. Go on! Back to the kitchen! We'll talk about this later.

(*The doorbell rings*)

ANTOINETTE. Oh, whenever you like.

(ANTOINETTE *exits up* c *and to* R. *The doorbell rings*)

ETIENNE. All right! Just coming. (*Moving up* c) This woman'll stick at nothing. I must keep her under close observation.

(*The doorbell rings*)

I'm coming.

(ETIENNE *exits* c. *After a moment* RAYMONDE *enters* c *and moves to the stool up* R. TOURNEL *follows and moves* L *above the table.* ETIENNE *follows to* c)

RAYMONDE. Didn't you hear us ringing?
ETIENNE. Yes, madame. I was coming . . .
RAYMONDE (*taking off her hat and gloves*) Monsieur Chandebise not back yet?
ETIENNE. What? Oh, no. No, madame.
RAYMONDE. All right. (*Turning to the stool*) You can go.
ETIENNE. Yes, madame. (*Turning up* c) You little—bitch!
TOURNEL. What did you say?
ETIENNE. I wasn't talking to you.

(ETIENNE *exits up* c, *closing the doors*)

TOURNEL. I should hope not. Well, my dear. Now I've seen you home—I think I'll be off.
RAYMONDE. You're not going to abandon me?
TOURNEL. Well . . .
RAYMONDE. Thank you very much! How do we know what Victor Emmanuel's next mood is going to be? You know when we met him in the hotel the second time? You may not have noticed, but he was trying to strangle you! Perhaps he's got a taste for it . . .
TOURNEL. You think I ought to stay?
RAYMONDE. I can't face him alone.
TOURNEL (*moving* R) Oh, all right! (*He sits on the sofa*)
RAYMONDE. You don't sound very keen on the idea.
TOURNEL. Are you surprised?
RAYMONDE. Men are all the same! (*Moving above the table* LC) Ready for anything except responsibility!

TOURNEL. Responsibility for what? Nothing happened . . .

RAYMONDE. It wasn't your fault nothing happened. (*Moving* c) And Victor Emmanuel doesn't know nothing happened. Finding us there he's quite entitled to think—whatever he thinks. And unless he thinks whatever he thinks why do you think he's so angry?

TOURNEL. What I can't understand is—why did he take so long to make up his mind—about what he thinks?

RAYMONDE (*moving* L) Well, yes.

TOURNEL. I mean, when he rolled in the first time, sitting on his bed, swigging vermouth . . .

RAYMONDE. Yes . . .

TOURNEL. He didn't seem so very shocked! He was really quite glad to see us.

RAYMONDE (*moving* L *of the sofa*) He even gave us a kiss!

TOURNEL. Exactly! And then—we see him again in that ridiculous cap and he leaps at my throat. I mean, in these little adventures one usually jumps to a conclusion right away. It's not something that needs mulling over . . . for hours and hours . . .

RAYMONDE. That's what I was thinking! It's most peculiar . . .

(*The doorbell rings.* TOURNEL *rises*)

My God—someone's at the door. Perhaps it's him.

TOURNEL. Already?

LUCIENNE (*off*) Is your mistress back?

ETIENNE (*off*) Yes, madame.

RAYMONDE (*moving up* c) No. It's Lucienne. (*Opening the door*) Come in!

(LUCIENNE *enters* c. TOURNEL *moves down* R)

LUCIENNE. Raymonde, darling. What dramas! (*She moves down* c)

RAYMONDE. Don't know it! (*She moves down* R *of Lucienne*)

LUCIENNE (*holding out her hand*) Look. I'm trembling like a leaf.

(RAYMONDE *takes Lucienne's hand.* TOURNEL *moves in* RC)

RAYMONDE ⎱ (*together*) Oh!
TOURNEL ⎰

LUCIENNE. And I can't go home. Never! Never! Oh, hullo, Monsieur Tournel. I'm sorry . . . (*She sits* R *of the table*)

TOURNEL. Don't mention it. Formalities later . . .

LUCIENNE. I'll sleep out under bridges—and railway embankments! Just as long as I never see that wild beast again! No! I should be too frightened to . . .

RAYMONDE. Oh, him! That's not a husband you've got, it's a tornado. When he saw us at the Hotel Coq d'Or, Monsieur Tournel and I—I really don't know what got into him; but he chased us with a revolver! Just as if he wanted to kill us.

TOURNEL. Yes, us! Would it be awfully inquisitive to ask why?

LUCIENNE (*rising*) You mean he was hunting you as well? It's too much . . . (*She moves below the table*)

TOURNEL. What a firebrand!

. . . . .

RAYMONDE. What a volcano!

LUCIENNE. I'm not out of the wood yet. Luckily your husband helped me to escape. Without him, God knows what'd have happened!

RAYMONDE. My husband?

LUCIENNE. *He* frightened me a bit, too.

RAYMONDE. Why?

LUCIENNE. I don't know if all the worry affected his mind . . .

RAYMONDE. You noticed it, too?

LUCIENNE (*moving* C *to Raymonde*) Most certainly I did! I mean he talked quite sensibly and begged me to go. Then oof! War broke out! We tumbled down the stairs, got to the bottom, and there he was looking most peculiar and saying, "Who is this Red Skin. Anyone you know?" "Do I know him? He's my husband," I said, "you know as well as I do!" And then he said, "Who are You? I don't know you." "Dear Heaven!" I said. "There he goes, poor old Victor Emmanuel, unhinged." Then he started talking gibberish, and I couldn't understand a syllable!

RAYMONDE. He did that to us!

TOURNEL. Exactly the same!

RAYMONDE. Insane!

TOURNEL. Afraid so . . .

LUCIENNE. And suddenly—I don't know what crossed his mind! He asked me to wet my whistle! Me! *Me!*

RAYMONDE }
TOURNEL   } (*together*) Oh!

LUCIENNE. "Now steady on," I said, "Chandebise." And he went, "Poche. Poche."

RAYMONDE }
TOURNEL   } (*together*) Yes. That's what he does. "Poche. Poche."

TOURNEL. It's his motto.

LUCIENNE. Well! Then, I'm afraid I got cold feet. I left your husband and I bolted. Oh, dear—I'm bolting still! (*She sits* R *of the table*)

RAYMONDE. Oh—what a day!

(*The doorbell rings.* LUCIENNE *rises*)

LUCIENNE. Someone—someone rang?

RAYMONDE }
TOURNEL   } (*together*) Yes.

TOURNEL. Perhaps it's—Chandebise!

RAYMONDE. That'd be odd! He's got a key.

TOURNEL. Sometimes he forgets it.

RAYMONDE. That's true.

TOURNEL. I well remember one time when old Chandebise forgot his key! It was winter, and the snow was coming down . . .

RAYMONDE. This is hardly the moment for reminiscences.

TOURNEL. Oh, all right.

RAYMONDE. Oh, help!

LUCIENNE. Isn't anyone going?

RAYMONDE. I don't know. But if someone rang . . .
TOURNEL. It probably means someone's at the door.
RAYMONDE. Obviously.
TOURNEL. All right.

(ETIENNE *enters up* C, *closing the doors*)

ETIENNE. Madame! Madame!

(TOURNEL *moves* R, RAYMONDE L *to the table*, LUCIENNE *below the table*)

RAYMONDE. Well? What is it?
ETIENNE. Oh dear, madame.
RAYMONDE. What?
ETIENNE. The master!
TOURNEL }
LUCIENNE } (*together*) Th . . .
RAYMONDE. Well?
ETIENNE. Well. I don't know what's the matter with the master.
I opened the door to him, and he came in like *this*, and said, "Is this
where Monsieur Chandebise lives?"
ALL. What?
ETIENNE. Yes, madame. Of course I thought, "Oh, dear me,
that's the master's little joke." I thought I'll join him in a bit of harm-
less fun, and I said, "Ha ha ha," I said, "certainly this is where
Monsieur Chandebise lives." But he didn't bat an eyelid. He just
said, "Will you tell him that I've come about the matter of my uni-
form."
ALL. No!
RAYMONDE. We're not going to start *that* all over again? Where is
he?
ETIENNE. In the hall. He's waiting . . .
TOURNEL }
LUCIENNE } (*together*) What?
RAYMONDE. He's *waiting?*
TOURNEL }
LUCIENNE } (*together*) In the hall?

(ETIENNE *opens the doors up* C)

RAYMONDE. Oh, for heaven's sake!

(RAYMONDE *moves up* R *of the door*, LUCIENNE L *of Etienne*, TOUR-
NEL R *of Raymonde*. POCHE *is seen sitting in the bench in the hall*)

ALL. Oh!
RAYMONDE. What on earth are you doing there?
POCHE. What did you say?
RAYMONDE. Waiting like a tradesman?
POCHE (*rising and moving down to the doorway*) Madame?
EVERYONE. "Madame?"
RAYMONDE. "Madame." Oh, do come in . . .
POCHE. I'm waiting for Monsieur Chandebise.

TOURNEL ⎱ (*together*) What?
LUCIENNE ⎰

RAYMONDE. What did you say?

ETIENNE. You see, madame. What did I tell you?

POCHE (*taking off his hat*) I remember you! I saw you, at the Hotel Coq d'Or. (*He slaps Etienne's chest with his hat*)

ETIENNE. Yes, sir. That's right.

POCHE. You're the chap whose wife . . .

ETIENNE. Oh, please, Monsieur . . .

RAYMONDE. What did he say?

POCHE. And you. You as well, madame! You're the lady from the hotel. You're the one that give us the cuddles, aren't you? All right, are you, madame? (*He lurches to Raymonde*)

RAYMONDE (*pushing Tournel below to Poche*) Oh, my God! Tournel! What's wrong with him?

TOURNEL. Steady on, old fellow.

POCHE. And the fancy man! How are you, darling? Give us a kiss!

TOURNEL (*pushing Poche away*) Now. That's quite enough of that, Victor Emmanuel! Victor Emmanuel!

POCHE (*moving* R *of the table* LC) No. Poche! I tell you Poche!

LUCIENNE (*moving* L *of the table*) You see. Poche. Poche. That's what he does.

POCHE. And you, madame! We were chased by redskins! Can you believe it! We were scared to death . . . (*He bangs the table with his hat*)

LUCIENNE (*running across* R *to Raymonde and holding her hand*) Yes—weren't we? Quite so . . .

POCHE. And all you birds—live together? In the same nest! Highly comical!

ALL. Oh . . .

(LUCIENNE *moves down* R, *leaving Raymonde between her and Tournel*)

POCHE (*moving* C) Did I say something wrong?

(ETIENNE *moves* L *of the sofa*)

ALL. No. Not at all. Nothing . . .

POCHE (*moving* L) Nice family—but a bit simple! (*He paces up and down* L)

RAYMONDE. But what's the matter with him?

LUCIENNE. Poor man. Let the doctor have a look at him.

ETIENNE. Shall I telephone Doctor Finache?

RAYMONDE. Oh, do what you like.

ETIENNE (*moving up* C) Yes, madame.

POCHE (*moving up* C) You off?

ETIENNE. Yes, sir. Yes . . .

POCHE. All right. But don't forget to tell Monsieur Chandebise.

LUCIENNE. Hear that?

ETIENNE. Yes, of course, sir. Yes, I will . . .

(ETIENNE *exits up* C)

TOURNEL. Is he playing charades?

RAYMONDE. He's working up to something!

POCHE (*moving down* c) You see my uniform was on the peg and . . .

LUCIENNE
TOURNEL } (*together*) Oh, yes? Really?

RAYMONDE. We've had quite enough of this!

POCHE. Ah . . .

RAYMONDE (*crossing below Tournel to Poche*) If you're ill for heaven's sake say so, and we'll get you taken care of. If it's a sort of game then it's very silly.

POCHE. Ah!

RAYMONDE. We've explained everything. We've proved it's mathematically impossible for anything to have gone on between me and Monsieur Tournel. Lucienne will bear us out.

LUCIENNE. Certainly!

RAYMONDE. That ought to be enough! So, if you persist in thinking—whatever you think—well, do as you like. After all Monsieur Tournel's here to answer for himself . . .

TOURNEL. Me?

POCHE. Oh!

RAYMONDE. Absolutely! So whether you believe us or not, at least rise to the occasion! Stop making an exhibition of yourself!

POCHE. Me?

RAYMONDE. Yes, you! When you're confronted with the evidence you take us in your arms and kiss us. Ten minutes later you're trying to strangle Monsieur Tournel!

POCHE. Did I try to strangle you?

TOURNEL. Yes.

RAYMONDE. Do you believe us or not?

POCHE. Of course I believe you.

RAYMONDE. Good! So let's have one big kiss and never mention it again! (*She opens her arms*)

POCHE (*wiping his mouth*) Why stop at one? (*He moves to Raymonde*)

ALL. At last!

RAYMONDE (*pushing Poche away to* R *of her*) Oh!

(POCHE *treads on Tournel's foot*)

TOURNEL. Ow!

ALL. What's the matter?

RAYMONDE. You've been drinking!

POCHE. What?

RAYMONDE. You smell of drink!

POCHE. Me?

RAYMONDE (*pushing Poche to Tournel*) Try a whiff of that!

TOURNEL. Overpowering! (*He moves down* LC)

RAYMONDE. So, you've taken to drink now, have you?

ALL. Oh . . . !

POCHE. What me? Drink? Just a couple of swallows to restore the bloodstream and so on. You know how it is. (*He slaps Raymonde's stomach with his hat*)

RAYMONDE. Tight! Completely tight! (*She moves up stage* L *of the sofa and leans on it*)

ALL. Oh . . . !

POCHE. Me? How could you say that? Not a word of truth! And you know it, my girl . . . (*He slaps her behind with his hat*)

RAYMONDE (*pushing Poche away to* LC) Go away. Go and sleep it off somewhere else.

POCHE. What?

TOURNEL. Oh, Victor Emmanuel! That you should sink so low . . .

POCHE (*right into Tournel's face*) No, no, Poche—I tell you, Poche!

TOURNEL. All right, if that's how you want it. (*He pushes Poche away down* R)

LUCIENNE. Oh . . . (*She moves up stage to Raymonde*)

POCHE. Yes! That's how I want it! Of course I do! If you all go on like this I'll get really angry.

(TOURNEL *moves below the table*)

RAYMONDE. It's disgusting!

(ETIENNE *enters up* C)

ETIENNE. Here's the doctor, madame.

(FINACHE *enters up* C)

ALL. *Ah* . . . !

FINACHE (*moving down* C) What's the matter? Etienne says he was just telephoning me. Hullo, Chandebise. (*He moves down* R *to Poche*)

POCHE. Where is this Chandebise?

(LUCIENNE *moves down* LC *to* R *of Tournel*)

FINACHE. Very witty! Ha ha. Yes. What's the matter?

RAYMONDE (*moving* LC, R *of Lucienne*) Just that the gentleman's dead drunk.

FINACHE. What? *Him!*

ETIENNE (*moving above the sofa,* L *end*) What? Monsieur Chandebise!

TOURNEL } (*together*) Yes.
LUCIENNE }

POCHE. What? *Me?*

RAYMONDE. Just take a sniff. Go on.

FINACHE. It's not true, is it, old man?

POCHE. *Me?* Pffh!

FINACHE. Oh . . . !

POCHE. They're joking!

FINACHE (*recoiling slightly*) Yes, indeed. Strong stuff!

ETIENNE. Oh, sir. *You* . . .

FINACHE. My poor, dear friend. What did you drink to get into a state like this?

POCHE. What? You as well! Look here, my good man . . .

FINACHE. My good man?

POCHE. You finished your little joke, have you? I'm no more tight than you are! (*Moving below the others to down* L)

FINACHE. All right. Now, then, old fellow . . .

POCHE. I tell you! (*In Tournel's face*) You're driving me out of my mind!

(TOURNEL *recoils a pace up stage*)

Ever since I came in at that door my head's been spinning round— (*in Lucienne's face*)—like a top!

(LUCIENNE *recoils a pace upstage*)

I don't know you! (*In Raymonde's face*) What are you trying to do, anyway?

(RAYMONDE *recoils a pace up stage*)

(*Moving across* R) I'm here to see Monsieur Chandebise, and—(*in Finache's face*)—Monsieur Chandebise I'll see. (*Moving down* R) I've nothing more to say. (*He paces up and down* R)

FINACHE. Oh dear, dear.

RAYMONDE. You see?

(ETIENNE *moves down in line with the others, to* R *of Finache*)

LUCIENNE. Just a few lucid flashes and then—pfft!

TOURNEL. He's been like that since this afternoon.

FINACHE. It's a serious attack.

RAYMONDE. Can you believe it?

(POCHE *turns the chair* R *to face the window*)

TOURNEL. What's he doing now?

(POCHE *makes a rude noise at the others, then sits*)

LUCIENNE ⎱ (*together*) Oh!
TOURNEL ⎰

FINACHE. Any previous disturbances?

RAYMONDE. Never. Isn't that right, Etienne?

ETIENNE. Never.

FINACHE. There are obviously strong hallucinatory symptoms. I would say—an amnesia of a very pronounced degree and a complete loss of contact with his true personality. One finds that with inveterate alcoholics.

ALL. No!

FINACHE. After this, we'll be getting delirium tremens.

ALL. Oh . . . !

(POCHE *rises, bangs the table with his hat, and sits again. They all gasp*)

RAYMONDE. It doesn't make sense! He only has one small glass of cognac after dinner.

TOURNEL. He often leaves half of it.

ETIENNE. And I have to finish it off, to prevent the waste . . .

LUCIENNE. One small glass wouldn't make him like that.

FINACHE. In some cases half a small glass of cognac is more than enough! Alcoholism isn't a question of amount, it depends on the idiosyncratic tendencies of the personality factor.

ALL (except Tournel) On the what?

FINACHE. The personality tends, in a greater or less degree . . .

TOURNEL (taking a pace down stage) Yes! To make an idiot of itself!

FINACHE. What? No—certainly not!

TOURNEL (taking a pace up stage) Oh? Sorry, I thought it did.

(As FINACHE speaks, the others huddle round him)

FINACHE. The personality factor regulates an individual's personal reactions. Some people can absorb a bottle a day--and it doesn't do them the slightest harm; others only need one little glass and poof . . . alcoholism!

POCHE. I bet they're saying something nasty about me.

FINACHE. And there, of course, lies the great danger. A glass of cognac after dinner? What's wrong with that? Nothing, apparently! Until the day of reckoning. And then—well, look at the pitiful result.

(They all form a line again as before and look at Poche)

ALL. Oh . . . !

POCHE (rising and moving down R) All right, you lousy string of onions! Enjoying yourselves?

ALL. What?

POCHE. You know what I mean! This has got to stop, or it'll all end in tears!

FINACHE (crossing below Etienne to Poche) What is it, my poor friend? What's the matter?

POCHE. I'm not a fool, you know!

FINACHE. There! There! (Moving to the others) Irritable with it, you see? One of the well-known symptoms.

POCHE. What?

FINACHE (moving back to Poche) Nothing, my dear fellow. Nothing at all. Now then, stretch out your hand.

POCHE. My hand?

FINACHE. Like this. (Holding out his hand) Can you manage that?

POCHE. What for? (He holds out a very shaky hand)

ALL. Oh. Look he's got the shakes!

FINACHE (moving to the others) You see that, the alcoholic tremor? Typical of the condition.

POCHE (stamping his foot) Ahaha! Ahaha! Ahaha!

ALL (recoiling two paces up stage) Ahaha?

POCHE (stamping across to down L and back) Stop it! Stop it! Stop it!

ALL. Oh, my God!

FINACHE. What's the trouble, old fellow?

POCHE (continuing to stamp about) You want to drive me loony, don't you? That's what you want to do!

ALL. No. Certainly not!

RAYMONDE. Please. (*Taking a pace down to Poche as he passes*) Keep calm, dear.

POCHE. Piss off! (*He moves down* L *and paces up and down*)

RAYMONDE. What did he say?

FINACHE. Take no notice. (*Moving up* R) They don't know what they're doing during these attacks. This way. We'll try not to excite him. (*He indicates the door up* R)

(LUCIENNE *and* RAYMONDE *move up stage*)

RAYMONDE. He's going too far! It's all jolly fine and large for him to be an alcoholic, but to tell me to pi . . . Is that what he told me to do?

FINACHE. What do you expect? He's over-excited. Leave me alone with Etienne. We'll try and get him to bed.

RAYMONDE. Yes. Put him to bed! Because really . . .

FINACHE. Yes. Yes. (*Showing Lucienne the door up* R) Pardon me, madame.

LUCIENNE. Of course. What a terrible thing—at his age!

(LUCIENNE *exits up* R)

FINACHE. Go along, Tournel.

TOURNEL (*moving up* C) Yes. You know, I once saw a very small alcoholic. He was about twelve years old! It was one summer . . .

RAYMONDE. For heaven's sake! Tell us another time!

(RAYMONDE *and* TOURNEL *exit up* R. FINACHE *and* ETIENNE *look at Poche, then at each other, they move down* C *level with Poche*)

FINACHE. Well now, my old friend . . .

POCHE. Good thing you got rid of them. It could've led to violence.

FINACHE (*moving to Poche below the table*) That's what I felt so strongly.

POCHE. What the hell's wrong with them all? Soft in the turnip?

FINACHE. Exactly. Soft. Yes, quite so. In the turnip.

POCHE (*crossing below Finache to Etienne; gesticulating*) What did I tell you?

(FINACHE *tries to hold Poche's gesticulating hand*)

ETIENNE. Soft, sir. In the turnip as you say.

POCHE. You should've tipped me the wink. You know, just whispered, "They're all cracked." Are you trying to hold my hand?

FINACHE. Pure friendship, old fellow.

POCHE. Oh, well—it's no good getting angry with them. You've got to humour the poor devils.

FINACHE. Damned odd. Hardly ticking over.

POCHE. What?

FINACHE. I've been listening to your pulse. Nothing doing. He's hardly ticking over.

POCHE. Of course not! (*Slapping Finache on the stomach with his hat*) No ticks on me at all! (*He moves below to* RC)

FINACHE (*following Poche*) Oh, riotously funny! Oh, yes, irresistible. (*He signs to Etienne to laugh*) Ha! Ha! Ha!

ETIENNE. Ha! Ha! Ha! Ha! Ha! (*He follows Finache*)

POCHE. At least we made the flunkey laugh!

FINACHE. Oh, yes. Very quick. Delightful pun! And now we've had a good laugh we must try and be sensible—again.

POCHE. What?

FINACHE. I'm your old friend. You know me.

POCHE. No!

FINACHE. All right. I'm the doctor! The nice, kind doctor! Who looks after you all! Little aches and pains? Touch of the collywobbles . . . That's when the Medicine Man comes to call.

POCHE. So, you're a doctor.

FINACHE. You've got it! (*He nods to Etienne*)

POCHE (*facing front*) Why is he acting so childish?

FINACHE. Now looking at you—I can tell—I can tell . . . You must be quite exhausted . . .

POCHE. Me?

FINACHE. Yes. You're exhausted. (*To Etienne*) He's exhausted!

POCHE. Exhausted! What do you expect? Up at five. Sweep out. Polish the floors. Lug up the logs . . .

FINACHE. Naturally. Naturally.

ETIENNE. Naturally. (*He takes a pace to* L)

POCHE. Naturally!

FINACHE. So why not get your clothes off and pop straight into bed?

POCHE (*moving below Finache to up* C) Bed? Certainly not!

FINACHE. All right. At least slip out of that jacket and let Etienne bring you a nice comfortable dressing-gown!

POCHE. All right. But my uniform . . .

FINACHE. Just while you're waiting for it to arrive. Etienne!

ETIENNE. Yes, Doctor.

(ETIENNE *exits down* L. FINACHE *takes Poche by the shoulders and sways him to and fro*)

FINACHE. Now. There we are! There's a lovely bed in there . . .

POCHE. Why can't he keep still?

FINACHE. Wouldn't you like to stretch out in there?

POCHE. He's making me seasick.

FINACHE. And have a delicious forty winks.

POCHE (*breaking free*) Me? Don't be stupid. What about Monsieur Chandebise?

FINACHE. Monsieur Chandebise? Oh! Good Heavens! If he says anything to you about it, come and tell me.

POCHE. Oh, all right . . .

(ETIENNE *enters* L *with a dressing-gown*)

ETIENNE. Here's the dressing-gown.

FINACHE (*turning Poche round and removing his jacket*) Now. Off with that nasty old jacket.

POCHE. This doesn't mean you've got permission to do just what you like with me!

(ETIENNE *helps* POCHE *to put on the dressing-gown*)

FINACHE. There's a good chap! Don't say that doesn't feel better.

POCHE. Do I look like the Pope at all?

FINACHE (*handing the jacket to Etienne*) There. You see . . .

(ETIENNE *puts the jacket on the chair above the table*)

POCHE. Better quality stuff than my uniform.

FINACHE. Certainly is! And now a little bird keeps telling me that you're getting thirsty.

POCHE. Oh. What a sly little bird!

FINACHE. Isn't she? So, I'm going to give you a little drink. It may taste just a tiny bit disgusting, but I want you to gulp it all down.

POCHE. Strong stuff?

FINACHE. What? Oh, yes—strong stuff . . .

POCHE (*moving to the sofa and sitting* L *end*) Come on then. I can manage it!

FINACHE. Good man. (*Moving* R *of Etienne*) You got some ammonia?

ETIENNE. I think so, sir.

POCHE. What a godsend!

FINACHE. Right. We'll give him ten drops in a glass of water.

ETIENNE. Yes, sir.

FINACHE. And when he comes to, you make him take—I'll give you a prescription . . .

ETIENNE. Yes, sir.

FINACHE. Where's something to write with?

ETIENNE (*pointing down* R) Over there.

FINACHE (*taking the chair* RC *to the desk down* R) Good. But first put him to bed. (*He sits*)

ETIENNE. Yes, Doctor. Now, sir. (*Moving to Poche*) If you'd like to step this way. Take my arm, sir.

(POCHE *rises and takes Etienne's arm. They move down* L)

POCHE. You're not a bad lad, are you?

(FINACHE *prepares to write*)

ETIENNE. You're very kind to say so, sir.

POCHE. Quite a decent individual in fact.

ETIENNE (*opening the door down* L) Thank you, sir, thank you very much.

POCHE. Pity you married a tart.

(POCHE *exits down* L. ETIENNE *follows*)

FINACHE. My God! What a stench! Talk about perfumed writing paper! Strong smell of maids' bedrooms! Must be Camille.

(CAMILLE *enters up* C *and closes the doors. He has not yet recovered the palate*)

CAMILLE. You—oh, Doctor! I'll never forget your hotel! What hasn't happened! (*He moves down* C)

FINACHE. Don't talk so fast.

CAMILLE. If you knew . . .

FINACHE. Put your palate in! After all the trouble I went to!

CAMILLE. I've lost my palate.

FINACHE. What?

CAMILLE. A horrible Hun person knocked it out when he punched me! In the chops!

FINACHE (*scarcely understanding*) A Hun punched you in the chops?

CAMILLE. If that'd been all. Oh, it's been a nightmare! And who did I happen to bump into? Tournel! And Raymonde! And Chandebise with a load of logs! Why a load of logs in the name of God! And Madame Homenides, and her husband after her with a pistol. Bang! Bang! I saw them all! What tragedies! My God! What disasters! (*He sits* R *of the table*)

(ANTOINETTE *enters up* R)

ANTOINETTE (*moving down* R) The mistress wants to know if the master's any better.

FINACHE (*rising and moving* C) Oh. Tell her he's a little better. No. I'll tell her myself . . .

CAMILLE. Now what's happened?

FINACHE. Nothing much. (*Moving up* R) Chandebise's a little under the weather.

CAMILLE. There you are!

(ETIENNE *enters down* L)

ETIENNE. He's in bed.

FINACHE. Good!

ETIENNE (*moving up* C) Good evening, Monsieur Camille.

CAMILLE. Hullo, Etienne.

FINACHE. Right, Etienne. Get the ammonia ready while I go and see your mistress.

(FINACHE *exits up* R, *followed by* ANTOINETTE)

ETIENNE. Yes, Doctor.

(ETIENNE *exits up* C. CAMILLE *rises to* C)

CAMILLE. Helpless! That's what I am! A useless pawn! A little bit of fluff, caught up in a whirlwind.

(*There is a knock on the door down* L)

(*Moving* R) Oh, come in! I'm about to lose my reason!

(POCHE *enters* L)

POCHE. Excuse me . . .

CAMILLE. Victor Emmanuel!

POCHE. Here's a young man I caught sight of at the Hotel Coq d'Or.

CAMILLE. Now for it . . .

POCHE (*moving below the table*) Another one, in fact.

CAMILLE. He recognized me! I'll explain. (*Moving* L *to Poche*) If I was there it was for a reason. As a matter of fact it was for a very good reason. I'd heard that a certain lady there . . .

POCHE. Got something stuck in his gullet.

CAMILLE. What?

POCHE (*slapping Camille on the back*) Cough it up, old man. Spit it out, whatever it is . . .

CAMILLE. I haven't got anything stuck in my gullet. I was telling you there was a lady there interested in life insurance.

POCHE. I'm not interested in all that. I'm dying of thirst. They said they'd bring me a drink but it's my view they've totally forgotten me.

CAMILLE. Who has?

POCHE. Hoo har?

CAMILLE. Hoo har!

POCHE. Oh, who has? Hoo har! The doctor.

CAMILLE. Oh. I'll see to it at once. (*He moves up stage*)

POCHE. You're a good lad!

(CAMILLE *turns.* POCHE *moves down* L, *winks and exits*)

CAMILLE. Good lad! Extraordinary. I thought I'd be covered with abuse. He almost congratulated me. I was wrong about Uncle Victor Emmanuel. (*Moving up* C) I thought the old boy had a narrow mind. It's as broad as can be. (*He sees Chandebise approaching and runs below the table* L) Ah!

(CHANDEBISE *enters up* C)

CHANDEBISE (*moving down* C) What is it?

CAMILLE. Oh, my God! There! There!

CHANDEBISE. What on earth?

(CAMILLE *bangs the table and moves up* C)

CAMILLE. I'm losing my reason!

CHANDEBISE (*following Camille up* C) Camille—for heaven's sake!

CAMILLE. I've gone mad! Mad . . .

(CAMILLE *exits up* C *and to* L)

CHANDEBISE. Delirious! It's infectious today. That hotel—what a nightmare! (*Seeing his jacket on the chair above the table*) My jacket! (*He takes off his uniform and hat and starts to put on his jacket, moving up* L *of the table*) I wonder who brought it back? At last I can get out of this ridiculous uniform. Having to come back in that get-up! The porter showed me to the servants' entrance!

(CAMILLE *enters up* C *from* L. ETIENNE *enters up* C *from* R)

CAMILLE. Etienne! I've gone mad . . .

(CAMILLE *exits up* R)

CHANDEBISE. Why does he keep doing that?
ETIENNE (*moving* C) What's the matter with Monsieur Camille?
CHANDEBISE. Etienne! I can't imagine.
ETIENNE. Sir! You recognize me!
CHANDEBISE. Don't be silly! Why shouldn't I recognize you?
ETIENNE (*moving to the doors up* C) No reason. Of course, sir. (*Stopping at the doors*) No reason at all.

(ETIENNE *makes a dignified exit* C. CAMILLE *enters up* R)

CAMILLE. There's two! I tell you. Two of them. Look. There! There!

(RAYMONDE, TOURNEL, FINACHE *and* LUCIENNE *enter up* R, *in that order*)

ALL (*as they enter*) What? Where?
CAMILLE. I'm mad! That's what it is. Mad!

(CAMILLE *exits up* C)

ALL. What's the matter with him?

(RAYMONDE *moves up* LC, LUCIENNE *to* L *of the tallboy*, FINACHE *to* R *of Lucienne*, TOURNEL R *of the sofa*, CHANDEBISE *up* L *of the table* L)

RAYMONDE. It's us, my dear. We've come to see you . . .
CHANDEBISE. You! Here, madame? And your paramour?
RAYMONDE ⎫
TOURNEL ⎬ (*together*) What?
         ⎭

(*During the following speeches*, CHANDEBISE *grabs Tournel by the lapels and pushes him round down stage of the table* L, *then up* L, *to up* C, *and to* L *of the sofa*. FINACHE *and* RAYMONDE *follow them, ending up in their former positions*. LUCIENNE *also follows, then remains* L *of the table*)

CHANDEBISE. So, what are you doing, eh? What were you doing when I caught you—in that disorderly house?
ALL. Oh!
RAYMONDE. Not again!
TOURNEL. But my dear chap, we've explained it a hundred times.
CHANDEBISE. Explained—what? Get out! You think you can go on pulling the wool over my eyes for ever! Out of my house!
RAYMONDE. Now, dear . . .
CHANDEBISE. Out of my house!
LUCIENNE. Look here, Monsieur Chandebise . . .
CHANDEBISE. Not you, dear lady. (*To Tournel*) But *you.* I never want to set eyes on you again! (*He moves down* R *and stands in front of the window*)
FINACHE. Come along, everyone. Don't excite him! He's clearly in the middle of a fit! You can come back when it's over.

RAYMONDE. His fits! I've really had enough of his fits . . .

(RAYMONDE *exits up* R)

FINACHE. Come along. Come along. Tournel. Please.

(LUCIENNE *exits up* R)

TOURNEL. He's berserk. Changes his mind every five minutes . . .

(TOURNEL *exits up* R)

FINACHE. Now then, my dear fellow. What's the matter now? (*He moves down* C)

CHANDEBISE. I'm sorry, Finache. I lost my temper!

FINACHE. It was an outlet for your inner frustrations. A catharsis! Probably did you good.

CHANDEBISE (*crossing* L *to below the table*) It should've done me good.

FINACHE. Of course. You're already a bit more rational. You can recognize people. You have an idea of your own identity.

CHANDEBISE. What?

FINACHE. You're coming on! Coming on!

CHANDEBISE. Recognize people—idea of my own identity . . . No. Not you, too!

FINACHE. What?

CHANDEBISE (*moving* C) Aren't I in the habit of recognizing people?

FINACHE. Oh, I wouldn't say you weren't but . . .

CHANDEBISE. I may lose my temper, but I'm not out of my head you know!

FINACHE. Of course not. Of course not . . .

CHANDEBISE. Ah. (*He moves below the table* L)

FINACHE. No, no, no, no no! All the same . . . not that it really matters, I don't think, we should have got out of bed quite so soon, should we?

CHANDEBISE. *What?*

FINACHE. And why did we have to put on our jacket again?

CHANDEBISE. Because I'm tired of running around looking like a commissionaire.

FINACHE. Like a com—commissionaire. Oh, I see . . .

CHANDEBISE (*moving* C) Perhaps you'd find it amusing to go about in fancy dress?

FINACHE. Oi, oi, oi! Oi, oi, oi!

CHANDEBISE (*moving below the table* L) But not me! I hate uniforms . . .

FINACHE. An obsession.

CHANDEBISE. I certainly saw life at your Hotel Coq d'Or.

FINACHE. You went there then?

CHANDEBISE. I went there!

FINACHE. You shouldn't have gone!

CHANDEBISE (*moving* C) Well, I went! What a joy-ride! Punched by one of them—kicked by another! The owner a raving maniac! He shoved me into uniform! Locked me into a room—so I had to escape across the roof! Nearly broke my neck! And to top the lot, Home-nides. Ho-me-ni-des! There can't be any disaster left! I've lived through them all! (*He moves* L)

FINACHE. Oh, my God. How sick he is!

(ETIENNE *enters with a glass of water and ammonia*)

CHANDEBISE. I'll never forget it . . .

ETIENNE (*moving down* R *of Finache*) Here we are!

CHANDEBISE. What have you got there, Etienne?

ETIENNE. Oh! Just something for the doctor.

FINACHE. Yes. For me.

CHANDEBISE. Oh, good.

FINACHE. Thanks. (*He puts some drops in the glass*)

(CHANDEBISE *paces up and down* L)

ETIENNE. Is it all right, Doctor?

FINACHE. Two—three—What?

ETIENNE. The master's better?

FINACHE. Afraid not.

ETIENNE. Not better?

FINACHE. Oh, dear, no. Six—seven . . .

ETIENNE. Oh . . .

FINACHE. Delirious. Quite delirious. Ten.

CHANDEBISE (*stopping below the table*) You in some sort of pain, Doctor?

FINACHE. No. No. (*Moving* L *to Chandebise with the glass*) Now. Drink this up!

CHANDEBISE. Me?

FINACHE. It'll set you up. After all you've gone through.

CHANDEBISE. All right. (*Taking the glass*) Losing my temper quite exhausted me.

FINACHE. Of course it did. All in one gulp now! You may find it a little strong . . .

CHANDEBISE. Oh, yes . . . (*He drinks as Finache instructs him*)

FINACHE. Big swallow now! Swallow! Don't say I didn't warn you! Down it goes . . . !

CHANDEBISE. Ah . . . (*He gasps, gives Finache the glass, runs to the window, opens it, and spits the liquid out*)

ETIENNE. Oh!

FINACHE (*running after Chandebise*) Oh!

CHANDEBISE. Doctor! I call that a joke, in quite appalling taste . . .

FINACHE. Look now, Chandebise.

CHANDEBISE (*pushing Finache aside and moving up* L) Oh, let me alone —you great oaf!

FINACHE (*moving* C) Where are you going?

CHANDEBISE. To wash my mouth out! Do you think I want to savour the bouquet?

(CHANDEBISE *exits up* L. *The doorbell rings*)

ETIENNE. Someone's ringing!

(ETIENNE *exits up* C)

FINACHE (*moving* L) All that work for nothing. He spat it out! (*He puts the glass on the table* L)
FERAILLON (*off*) Is Monsieur Chandebise at home?
ETIENNE (*off*) This way, sir.
FINACHE (*moving* C) Good heavens—Feraillon . . .

(FERAILLON *appears at the door up* C)

FERAILLON. Doctor!

(ETIENNE *appears behind Feraillon*)

FINACHE. Come in then.
FERAILLON. May I? (*He moves down* L *of Finache*)

(ETIENNE *closes the doors and moves* L *of Feraillon*)

FINACHE. Did you call about your insurance?
FERAILLON. Not that, Doctor. Any time'll do for that. (*Producing the palate*) No. I found this—object—in my hotel, which I take to be the property of Monsieur Camille Chandebise.
ETIENNE. *I* found that—I . . .
FERAILLON. Sir?
ETIENNE. I'm Etienne. Monsieur Chandebise's butler. (*He moves* L)
FERAILLON. Charmed, naturally.
FINACHE. Show me. It's his palate! He lost it when he went out! How did you deduce it was his?
FERAILLON (*moving a pace* L) It's got his name and address on it.
FINACHE. No! Oh, yes. Camille Chandebise, Ninety-five Boulevard Malesherbes. Clever idea that!
FERAILLON. Must be useful. If you've run out of visiting cards you just—leave the roof of your mouth . . .
FINACHE. I'll give it to him. He'll be relieved.

(ANTOINETTE *enters up* C *and moves between Feraillon and Finache*)

ANTOINETTE. Doctor! Doctor! Something's come over Monsieur Camille. I found him in the bathroom stark naked, in a cold shower. Singing the *Marseillaise*.

(ANTOINETTE *and* ETIENNE *move up* C *and talk*)

FINACHE. Well, whatever next!
FERAILLON. The *Marseillaise!*
FINACHE. You're right. It's madness! You see how he carries on, your precious Monsieur Camille? Singing the *Marseillaise* in the shower! No-one has any sense. (*Moving up* C) Where is he?
ANTOINETTE. This way, Doctor.

(ANTOINETTE *exits up* C *and to* L)

FINACHE. There's a plague in this house. Take me to the bathroom.

(FINACHE *exits up* c *and to* L)

FERAILLON (*moving above the table* L) The *Marseillaise* under a cold shower? Curious behaviour! (*Picking up the cap and showing it to Etienne*) Poche's uniform, if I'm not very much mistaken! Beautiful cap this—but what's it doing here? Has my porter been around here?

(CHANDEBISE *enters up* L *and moves down* L)

ETIENNE. Your porter? No, why?
FERAILLON. My God—there he is!
CHANDEBISE. Revolting taste!
FERAILLON. Here, Poche. Just you come here!
CHANDEBISE. The maniac! In my house! (*He runs up* L)

(FERAILLON *runs up* c. *During the following dialogue* CHANDEBISE *runs down* L, FERAILLON *runs down* L. CHANDEBISE *moves to* c *and is caught by* FERAILLON *below the table. They turn round twice, and* ETIENNE *moves between them. Eventually* CHANDEBISE *breaks away and runs up* c)

FERAILLON. Oh, you great animal! What're you doing here?
CHANDEBISE. Oh, help! Help—help!
FERAILLON. So—proud of your uniform, are you?
CHANDEBISE. Help! Help!
ETIENNE. Sir! What are you doing?
FERALLION. Dismiss!
CHANDEBISE. No! Help! Help! Help! Hold him tight!

(CHANDEBISE *exits up* c, *closing the doors.* ETIENNE *holds Feraillon*)

FERAILLON. Just let me go. (*He breaks from Etienne and moves up stage, picking up the hat and coat from the table*)

(*There is a door-slam off up* L)

ETIENNE. That's Monsieur Chandebise, my master!
FERAILLON. That's your master? It's my servant! I know him of old.

(FERAILLON *exits up* c)

ETIENNE. No, it's not! It's not!

(ETIENNE *exits up* c, *closing the doors. There is another door-slam off* L. CHANDEBISE *enters up* R)

CHANDEBISE. Is the coast clear? I had the happy idea of banging the front door. He thinks I've gone out and he's busy chasing me down the street. (*He sits* L *on the sofa*) Thank God, he's gone.
ETIENNE (*off* c) I will announce you, sir, as is my custom.
HOMENIDES (*off* c) I will go in! I tell you, I will pass!
CHANDEBISE (*rising*) What's happening?

(HOMENIDES *enters* c *and moves down* c)

HOMENIDES. Him!

CHANDEBISE. Homenides! (*He starts to move down* R)

HOMENIDES. Don't move!

CHANDEBISE (*turning to face him*) How are you, dear friend?

HOMENIDES. Not dear friend any more! (*He takes off his hat and puts it with his stick and gloves on the sofa*) You have escaped so far. But now we face each other. If it hadn't been for the idiots who took me to the police station—you might have already made the acquaintance of a revolver! But the police inspector took it away. He made me swear—never to use a revolver again! I gave him—my word of honour!

CHANDEBISE. You did? Very sensible. A sound fellow, that police inspector.

HOMENIDES. My word of honour—no revolvers! So now I have brought pistols instead. (*He pulls out two pistols*)

CHANDEBISE. What?

HOMENIDES. Don't worry! I'm not going to slay you now. The moment for that was when I found you having—what do you French call it?—a *flagrante delighto*.

CHANDEBISE. I know what you mean.

HOMENIDES. Now it would be murder! That would be dangerous.

CHANDEBISE. I quite agree.

HOMENIDES. I have here—two pistols. One loaded—one not.

CHANDEBISE (*stepping to Homenides*) Good! I'll take the first one . . .

HOMENIDES. Oi—gar!

(CHANDEBISE *steps back*)

(*Taking a piece of chalk from his pocket and moving to Chandebise*) I take the chalk—and just draw a circle round your heart.

CHANDEBISE. Please—my best suit!

HOMENIDES (*backing below* L *of the sofa*) I do just the same! (*He makes a circle on his own heart*)

CHANDEBISE. He must be a tailor.

HOMENIDES. We each take a pistol and fire at the bull's-eye! (*Levelling the first pistol*) Bang! (*He levels the second pistol*) Whoever gets the bullet—*muerte!* Dead!

CHANDEBISE (*moving to Homenides*) What about the other one? (*He steps back*)

HOMENIDES. And so—we duel in my country.

CHANDEBISE. Most interesting, but . . .

HOMENIDES (*moving to Chandebise*) Take one.

CHANDEBISE. What?

HOMENIDES. Take one, I tell you! Take one!

CHANDEBISE (*backing below him to* C) I never take anything between meals!

HOMENIDES (*moving to Chandebise*) Take one! Or I'll kill you!

CHANDEBISE (*moving up* C) He's not joking! Oh, my God—help! Help!

(CHANDEBISE *exits up* C, *closing the doors*)

HOMENIDES (*following*) Chandebise. Will you come back! *Will you!*

(HOMENIDES *exits up* C, *leaving the doors open*)

CHANDEBISE (*off*) Help! Help!

HOMENIDES (*off*) Come back! Wait . . .

(CHANDEBISE *enters up* R)

CHANDEBISE (*running down* L) Help! Help! Aaah! I'm asleep in my bed! We're haunted, the house is full of spirits . . .

(CHANDEBISE *exits down* L, *then re-enters and runs up* C. HOMENIDES *enters up* R, *moves* C, *then turns back to lock the door up* R)

HOMENIDES (*as he enters*) Where is the miserable coward—wait a minute, wait a . . .

CHANDEBISE. Help! Help!

(CHANDEBISE *exits up* C, *shutting the doors*)

HOMENIDES (*moving to the doors up* C, *finding them locked, and banging on them*) Open, miserable coward! Will you open—hey, Chandebise! You think you're safe because you lock the door, but you don't know me. When I set out to do something I see it though to the end, and if I have to break down every door in the house I shall do it. You hear me, Chandebise? I'm going to break down the . . .

(POCHE *enters down* L *and moves* C)

POCHE. Who's making all this noise? How do you expect me to sleep?

(HOMENIDES *runs down* L, *locks the door, and moves below the table*)

HOMENIDES. You won't escape me now.

POCHE. My God, the redskin!

HOMENIDES (*holding out the pistols*) Take one, so I can kill you!

POCHE (*running up* C) What? Help! Help! (*He tries the* C *doors, then the door up* R)

(*During the following dialogue,* HOMENIDES *moves up* C *then down* R. POCHE *moves to the sofa.* HOMENIDES *chases him round it.* POCHE *exits through the french window and dives off the balcony*)

HOMENIDES. Stand your ground!

POCHE. Help! Help!

HOMENIDES. Take your medicine!

POCHE. Medicine! Help! Help!

HOMENIDES. Advance two paces and fire!

POCHE. Help! Help! Help! Aaaaaahh!

(HOMENIDES *follows Poche to the window and looks out*)

HOMENIDES. Oh, poor man—he's going to kill himself! No! He's all right. So—I'll kill him! Si! Slay him! (*Moving* C) I need a drink. (*He moves to the table* L, *picks up the glass, and drinks*) Ah! Porrah! (*He runs to the window and spits it out*) Another filthy French drink! (*He*

moves to the desk and leans on the chair in front of it) A filthy French perfume! The perfume of the letter. The perfume of my wife. (*He picks up
a piece of notepaper*) The paper's the same. And her writing. (*Reading*)
"Dear Sir, having noticed you the other evening at the Palais
Royal . . ." The twin brother of the letter to the husband. Why is it
here? In Senora Chandebise's writing-case? (*Moving up* R, *unlocking
the door and knocking*) I want to know!

(TOURNEL *enters up* R)

TOURNEL. What do you want?
HOMENIDES (*grabbing Tournel by the lapels and swinging him round* L)
I want to know!
TOURNEL. Stop it! No more cowboys and Indians.
HOMENIDES. The letter!
TOURNEL. Oh, let me go!

(RAYMONDE *enters up* R)

RAYMONDE (*moving* C) Now what is it?
HOMENIDES (*pushing Tournel to* L *of the table and turning to face
Raymonde*) No—you! I found the letter in your papers.
RAYMONDE. You've been rifling my letters!
HOMENIDES. And found my wife's handwriting! That's the point.
Why?
RAYMONDE. Well, now . . .
HOMENIDES. This is where she makes up love letters!
RAYMONDE. Yes. This is where she does it! And then you go and
get hold of the wrong end of the stick. Now you can see—it's all quite
innocent.
HOMENIDES. So—ow?
RAYMONDE. What do you mean: "so—ow?" Do you think if she
was carrying on a secret romance with my husband I'd let her write
to him on my mauve writing-paper? (*She moves down* R)
TOURNEL (*moving down* L) Out of her writing-case?

(LUCIENNE *enters up* R)

HOMENIDES. Egthplain!
RAYMONDE. Egthplain. Egthplain. Here's your wife! Ask her
yourself!
HOMENIDES (*moving up stage to Lucienne*) Tell me, madame . . .
LUCIENNE. My husband!
HOMENIDES (*bringing Lucienne down* C) Please. Wait a moment.
With one word—you can bring peace to my heart. The letter—that
letter!
LUCIENNE. What?
HOMENIDES. I found it *there*. (*He points to the desk*) Why?
LUCIENNE. It's not my secret.
RAYMONDE. Oh, tell him the answer to the riddle! He's like a bear
with a sore head.
LUCIENNE. You want me to?
RAYMONDE. Go on.

LUCIENNE. All right. You're as bad as Othello and that stupid handkerchief! Couldn't you understand? What a clown the man is! Raimunda creia tener motivo de dudar de la fidelidad de su marido. (*Raymonde thought her husband was unfaithful*)
HOMENIDES. Como? (*Why?*)
LUCIENNE. Entonces para probarlo decidio darle una cita galante —al la cual ella tambien asistiria. (*For proof she arranged a meeting to which she would go as well*)
HOMENIDES. Pero, la carta! La carta! (*But the letter, the letter*)
LUCIENNE. Ah! La carta! La carta! Espera, hombre! Si ella hubiese escrito la carta a su marido, este hubiera reconocido su escriture. (*Ah! The letter! The letter! Wait, man! Had she written the letter to her husband, he would have recognized the writing*)
HOMENIDES. Despues! Despues! (*After! After!*)
LUCIENNE. Entonces ella me ha encargado de escribir en su lugar. (*She asked me to write for her*) Ask Raymonde.
HOMENIDES (*moving* R *to Raymonde*) Es verdad? Es verdad? (*That is true? That is true?*)
RAYMONDE. Yes. What did you say exactly?
HOMENIDES. Es verdad lo que ella dice? (*Is it true what she says?*)
RAYMONDE. It's all as verdad as can be. What have I got to lose?
HOMENIDES (*kissing Raymonde's hand*) Ah, Senora, Senora! Quando pienso que me metido tantas ideas en la cabeza! (*When I think I put so many ideas in my head*)
RAYMONDE. Please. Don't mention it!
HOMENIDES (*moving to Lucienne*) Que estupido! (*He moves to Tournel*) Ah! Soy un bruto! Un bruto! Un bruto! (*How stupid! I am a brute! A brute! A brute!*)
TOURNEL (*facing front*) A man could do himself a fatal injury, talking to himself like that.

(LUCIENNE *hands Homenides' hat and stick to Raymonde, and stands below the sofa.* HOMENIDES *moves* C *and takes Lucienne's hand.* RAYMONDE *puts the hat and stick on the chair down* R)

HOMENIDES. Ah! Querida! Perdoname mis estrupideces. (*Ah, darling! Forgive my stupidity*)
LUCIENNE. Te perdono (*I forgive you*), but don't do it again!

(HOMENIDES *and* LUCIENNE *sit on the sofa*)

HOMENIDES. Ah! Querida mia! Ah. Yo te quiero. (*Ah! My darling! I love you*) (*He kisses Lucienne's hand*)
RAYMONDE. How quickly people understand each other, in Spanish!

(FINACHE, CAMILLE, CHANDEBISE *and* ETIENNE *enter up* C, *in that order.* FINACHE *moves to the table* L. CAMILLE R *of the table,* CHANDEBISE L *of the table,* ETIENNE, *leaving the doors open, stands* R *of them.* CAMILLE *is now wearing the palate*)

FINACHE. Be sensible, you know you've taken leave of your senses.

CAMILLE. I tell you I saw them at the same time. (*Pointing*) There and there!

CHANDEBISE. And I came face to face with myself! I was in my room. I saw me in my bed!

FINACHE. Oh, yes?

(TOURNEL *moves* RC, *above the chair* R *of the table*)

HOMENIDES. What's that? What?

CHANDEBISE. You—still here? (*He moves down* L *and stops*)

HOMENIDES. Don't worry. At the moment I am calm. I know my wife wasn't the stranger at the Palais. She didn't write you a love letter. It was yours!

CHANDEBISE (*to Raymonde*) What—you?

RAYMONDE. That's the fourteenth time you've been told. (*She moves* R *above the sofa*)

CHANDEBISE. What?

TOURNEL. And each time we kiss each other—to absolutely no effect. (*He bangs the chair on the floor and moves above the sofa to Raymonde*)

(RAYMONDE *and* TOURNEL *face up stage*)

CHANDEBISE. What's he say?

HOMENIDES. And for that—I made you go and jump out of the window . . .

(RAYMONDE *and* TOURNEL *face down stage*)

ALL. Out of the window?

HOMENIDES. Ah—then I felt a moment of pity for you!

CHANDEBISE (*moving up stage to Homenides*) *You* made *me* jump out of the window?

HOMENIDES. Of course I made you! You ran out of there. And hoop la! Through the window.

CHANDEBISE. Yes! Yes! You as well. (*Moving below the table* L) We're all the victims of the same extraordinary hallucination! What you saw jumping out of the window was what I saw on my bed—me!

CAMILLE. And what I saw—there and there!

CHANDEBISE. And it's proved by the fact that I never—absolutely never in any circumstances—jumped out of the window!

HOMENIDES. What are you trying to tell us?

FINACHE. It's beginning to tell on me. I knew it would.

TOURNEL (*moving down stage a pace*) We're bewitched!

(FERAILLON *enters up* C, *with Chandebises' dressing-gown*)

FERAILLON. Excuse me, ladies and gentlemen . . .

CHANDEBRISE (*dropping on all fours and crawling under the table*) The maniac!

FINACHE			Feraillon!
CAMILLE	}	(*together*) {	Feraillon!
RAYMONDE			(*moving down* R) The proprietor!
TOURNEL			(*moving down* R) From the hotel!

FERAILLON. I was just walking down the street when my hall porter happened to drop on my head. I can offer no explanation . . .
ALL. What?

TOURNEL ⎤
CAMILLE ⎬ (*together*) It was the porter!
HOMENIDES ⎦

FERAILLON (*moving downstage*) It would appear he jumped through a window, wearing this article of clothing . . . (*He holds out the dressing-gown*)
RAYMONDE. That's my husband's! (*Crossing below them all to down L*) It's yours, dear. Where's he got to? Victor Emmanuel! Victor Emmanuel!

(FINACHE *and* CAMILLE *open the door up* L *and call.* ETIENNE *opens the door up* C *and calls.* TOURNEL *goes to the french window and calls.* CHANDEBISE *crawls half out and tries to hush Raymonde*)

ALL. Victor Emmanuel!
FERAILLON (*seeing Chandebise*) Ah! (*He moves* L, *puts the dressing-gown on the table, and hauls Chandebise out by the collar*)
ALL (*slamming their various doors and turning on stage*) What?
FERAILLON. Poche! Poche again!
ALL. What do you mean, Poche?
CHANDEBISE. Ah—help! Help!
FERAILLON (*kicking Chandebise round in a circle down* RC) You scoundrel—you beastly individual! You low form of humanity! You —pig's abortion . . .

(FERAILLON *finishes kicking Chandebise when he is* C *and* CHANDEBISE *is* L)

ALL. Ah!

(RAYMONDE *moves between Feraillon and Chandebise. Everyone comes down stage, except* ETIENNE. *They form a line in the following order,* R *to* L, TOURNEL, LUCIENNE. HOMENIDES, FERAILLON, RAYMONDE, CHANDEBISE, CAMILLE, FINACHE)

RAYMONDE. Excuse me, sir! You're referring to my husband!
FERAILLON. What?
CHANDEBISE. He's got an obsession. Every time we meet he kicks me round in a circle!
FERAILLON. Him! Your husband?
RAYMONDE. Exactly. Monsieur Chandebise!
FERAILLON. He's the spitting image of my hall porter! Monsieur Poche!
ALL. Poche!
RAYMONDE. And the one we saw in the hotel swigging vermouth . . .
TOURNEL. Who kissed us . . .
ALL. That was Poche!
LUCIENNE. And the one who wanted me to wet my whistle . . .
CAMILLE. Who carried the load of logs . . .

ALL. That was Poche!

CHANDEBISE. Poche! Poche! Nothing but Poche. I'm sorry he left in such a hurry. I'd like to have seen him close to. My second self!

FERAILLON. We can arrange that—call in any day. At the Hotel Coq d'Or.

CHANDEBISE. No, thank you very much! I've seen quite enough of the Hotel Coq d'Or!

(RAYMONDE *steps one pace down stage*, CHANDEBISE *joins her*. FERAILLON, HOMENIDES, LUCIENNE *and* TOURNEL *form a group below the fireplace*, FINACHE *below it*. ETIENNE *exits up* C)

RAYMONDE (*teasing Chandebise*) Not even to meet a lovely stranger from the Palais Royal?

CHANDEBISE. You may mock! But who started this whole ridiculous ball rolling?

RAYMONDE. I'm sorry! Really I'm sorry! But what could I do? I thought you were unfaithful to me . . .

CHANDEBISE. Good heavens! Why? Whatever gave you that idea?

RAYMONDE. Well, because you—because . . .

CHANDEBISE. No! Not for such a little . . .

RAYMONDE. But *because* there was such a little . . .

CHANDEBISE. Oh—well!

RAYMONDE. I know. I was very silly. The fact is—I had a flea in my ear!

CHANDEBISE (*putting his* R *arm round her*) All right! I'll squash that flea, tonight!

RAYMONDE. You?

CHANDEBISE. Yes. That is—(*he lets her go*)—well, at least I'll try!

(TOURNEL *leaves the group by the sofa and moves down* C)

TOURNEL. Listen to this. You'll never believe it—not in a million years—but I must tell you . . .

ALL. Oh, no—save it up! Till tomorrow! Till tomorrow!

The lights BLACK-OUT *and*—

the CURTAIN *falls*

FURNITURE AND PROPERTY LIST

ACT I

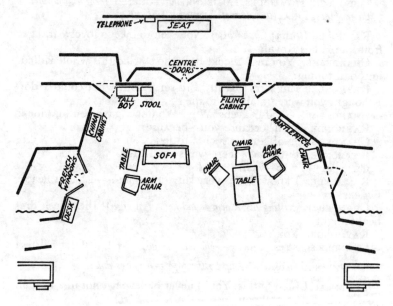

On stage: Portable writing desk (down R) *In it:* white writing paper, mauve
         writing paper, pen, ink, envelopes, blotter
        Cabinet (up R) *In it:* china. *On it:* white writing paper in box
        Occasional table (RC)
        Armchair (RC)
        Sofa (RC)
        Table (LC)
        Armchair (L of table LC)
        Chair (above table LC)
        Chair (R of table LC)
        Tallboy (up RC) *On it:* vase of flowers. *In drawer:* box
        Stool (up RC)
        Filing cabinet (up LC) *In it:* files
        Seat (in hall up C)
        On wall in hall: telephone
        On mantelpiece: vase of flowers, candlesticks
        On wall above window R: bellpush
        Carpet
        Window curtains

Off stage: Certificate (FINACHE)
File (CAMILLE)
Bottle of perfume (ANTOINETTE)
Brief-case with documents (TOURNEL)
Box with palate (FINACHE)
Glass (CAMILLE)
Bottle of boracic acid (CAMILLE)
Revolver (HOMENIDES)

Personal: RAYMONDE: handbag containing pair of braces

ACT II

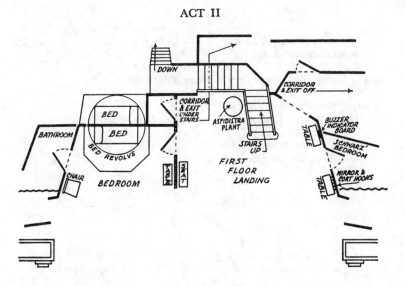

On stage: HALL:
Table (up L)
Table (down L)
Seat (down C)
Above table up L: buzzer indicator board
Above table down L: mirror, coat-hooks with uniform hat and coat
In curve of stairs: aspidistra

BEDROOMS:
Double revolving bed with bedding, pillows on R end of down-
stage bed, on L end of upstage bed
Chair (down R)
Table (down C)
On wall L *and* R *of beds:* push buttons

Stair carpet
Hall rug
Bedroom rug

Off stage: Feather duster (EUGÉNIE)
Bundle of linen (OLYMPE)
Jug (EUGÉNIE)
Telegram (OLYMPE)
Telegram (POCHE)
Log basket and logs (POCHE)
Bottle of vermouth (POCHE)

ACT III

Set: ANTOINETTE's apron on sofa
Magazines on table L

Check: Writing desk open. *On it:* written notepaper

Off stage: Dressing-gown (ETIENNE)
Tray with glass of water and bottle of ammonia (ETIENNE)
Palate (FERAILLON)
2 pistols (HOMENIDES)
Piece of chalk (HOMENIDES)

LIGHTING PLOT

Property fittings required: gas bracket (2 sets) 2 interior sets: a drawing-room; a combined hotel hall and bedroom

THE APPARENT SOURCES OF LIGHT:

Drawing-room; by day, french windows R; by night, gas brackets

Hall and bedroom, gas brackets

THE MAIN ACTING AREAS extend, in both sets, over the entire stage

ACT I. Afternoon

To open: Effect of afternoon light

Cue 1   CAMILLE: "Monsieur Tournel!" (End of act)   (Page 28)
Black-Out

ACT II. Night

To open: Brackets lit

Cue 2   End of Act   (Page 59)
Black-Out

ACT III. Night

To open: Brackets lit. Blue outside window

Cue 3   ALL: "Till tomorrow!" (End of Act)   (Page 87)
Black-Out

EFFECTS PLOT

ACT I

ACT II

ACT III

MADE AND PRINTED IN GREAT BRITAIN BY
LATIMER TREND & COMPANY LTD PLYMOUTH